"The limits of my language
are the limits of my world."

—— Ludwig Wittgenstein

SEVEN
AMERICAN
DEATHS
AND
DISASTERS

KENNETH
GOLDSMITH

powerHouse Books

BROOKLYN, NY

Seven American Deaths and Disasters

Text © 2013 Kenneth Goldsmith

Published in the United States by powerHouse Books, a division of powerHouse Cultural Entertainment, Inc.

37 Main Street, Brooklyn, NY 11201-1021
Tel.: 212.604.9074 Fax: 212.366.5247
info@powerhousebooks.com
www.powerhousebooks.com

First edition, 2013

Library of Congress Control Number: 2012953462

ISBN: 978-1-57687-636-7

Book design by Krzysztof Poluchowicz

Printed and bound Friesens Corporation, Altona, Manitoba, Canada

10 9 8 7 6 5 4 3

Printed in Canada

CONTENTS:

FOR CHRISTIAN BÖK

John F. Kennedy

See The Wheeler Dealers.

God bless you sir.

That's alright, buddy. We all feel the same. Anybody who has the courage to marry somebody named Eunice can't be all bad.

See The Wheeler Dealers, won't you? Now showing at two theaters in downtown Dallas, the Capri downtown Dallas and The Hollywood in downtown Fort Worth. Don't forget, President Kennedy's speech today has been billed as a major event. KLIF news, of course, will be bringing you excerpts of that speech throughout the afternoon. OK? I'm Andy Fine and away we go on the Rex Jones show.

The first of the two most glorious holidays of the year is coming. So it won't be long until you make a most important meat purchase. Yes, Thanksgiving is only days away and this happy holiday will be just a little better this year if a little forethought goes into the purchase of a traditional turkey. Naturally, you want a turkey that gives you extra meat per pound. And if you're like most families, you'll want a turkey that offers the most sweet, absolutely delicious white meat per pound. There are turkeys that meet these requirements. You'll find them at your grocer's bearing the famous Armour star. Yes, ma'am, I'm talking about Armour Star broad breasted turkeys, government inspected and graded to give your family a very special treat this Thanksgiving. Armour Star turkeys have moderately deep, well-rounded breasts with extra white meat, plenty of dark meat too. When you shop at your grocer's for that Thanksgiving turkey, get an Armour Star broad breasted turkey. Government inspected and graded to assure you of the very best. Armour Star, best by far.

I know what he's talking about. Twenty-two-and-a-half minutes now away from one o'clock. Alright, now let's take a little bit of time out here. Everybody to the icebox, let's get a beer.

The teams are on the field, the game time's here. Let's kick off the fun with a Falstaff beer. A great teammate for all your good times. Premium quality Falstaff, coast-to-coast for the most refreshing taste in beer, this is the one. Light, brisk Falstaff. For extra convenience, buy Falstaff in no deposit, no return cans in handy packs of six. Falstaff. This is the one.

(Boom-sh-boom)
(Boom-sh-boom)
(Boom-sh-boom)
(Boom)
I have a boyfriend
(Boom-sh-boom)
(Boom-sh-boom)
(Boom-sh-boom)
Met him a week ago
(Boom-sh-boom)
(Boom-sh-boom)
He's my forever
(Boom-sh-boom)

(Boom-sh-boom)
(Boom-sh-boom)
Last night he told me so
He's the boy that I adore
Never felt like this before
And I know I'll never let him go
I have a boyfriend
(Boom-sh-boom)
(Boom)
(Whoo-eee-whoo)
We'll never say goodbye
(Boom-sh-boom)
(Boom-sh-boom)
He made a promise
(Boom)
(Whoo-eee-whoo)
He'll never make me cry
(Boom-sh-boom)
Every time we kiss goodnight
Feels so good to hold him tight...

This is a KLIF bulletin from Dallas. Three shots reportedly were fired at the motorcade of President Kennedy today near the downtown section. KLIF news is checking out the report. We will have further reports. Stay tuned.

...up in the sky
(And someday I know) oh-oh, yeah
(We'll walk down the aisle)
Yes, we will (so much in love)
Whoa-oh-oh-oh (wearing a smile)
Every time we kiss goodnight
Feels so good to hold him tight
Oh-oh, I'm so glad I have a boyfriend
I have a boyfriend

Whoa-oh-oh-oh-oh, whoa-oh-oh-oh
I have a boyfriend, yeaaaaah, I do

Oh yeah, I Have A Boyfriend is the name of that one by The Chiffons. And I think that is a real winner. As a matter of fact, you must think so too, already voted number thirty-six on the instant Top Forty on KLIF.

We're doing our Christmas shopping at Robert Hall
this year.

We're saving on clothes for Christmas at Robert Hall
this year.

More quality for low prices
On gifts for one and all.
There's a wide selection,
A bigger collection
Where America goes for family clothes,
It's Robert Hall this year.

For the lady who wants more fashion at less cost, Robert Hall has a delightful array of holiday dresses priced as low as $7.97. Other Christmas features are the elegant three-piece wool suits priced from only $12.97. Robes and pajama sets are priced from only $3.97 at Robert Hall, gift center for the family.

You bet your sweet life. Hey fellas, get the aristocrat suit, the Julliard worsted suit, nationally advertised in Look and Life magazine. Robert Hall now features the Julliard suit at just $46.95. Don't forget. Alterations definitely are included.

KLIF 1190.

Hello, we have sixty-three degrees in Big D at the moment, going up too...

The best meat from the farmer goes to Armour and from Armour to the butcher to you. If you want the best from the farmer ask for Armour and do what the butchers do. Be sure it's Armour, the meat the butcher brings home.

Say, if you fix lunches for the family every day, there's a mighty happy solution to the variety problem. Armour Star lunch meat. Why, there are so many varieties, you could go for a couple of weeks without ever repeating. Nourishing? Four slices of Armour lunch meat in a couple of sandwiches pack all the wallop of a bowl of beef stew. Get Armour Star lunch meat for the kids. The sandwich meat that sticks to your ribs. Lots of different kinds. Easy to make. So for goodness sake, be sure it's Armour. The meat the butcher brings home.

Six minutes away from the hour of one o'clock right now on the Rex Jones show. This is Tommy Roe. He includes just about everybody.

Everybody, everybody,
Everybody's, had a broken heart now...

Here is a further report after we have just received word that shots have been fired at the Kennedy motorcade. We just talked to the police department. Here is that conversation.

Several persons arrived at Parkland and no information is being given at this time.

But you did have a report of shots being fired.

We have reports, yes sir.

KLIF news. On at Parkland Hospital to confirm the reports that someone had been wounded in the firing of shots in the Kennedy motorcade at downtown Dallas. Stay tuned for more news.

...everybody, everybody,
everybody's blue when they're lonesome.
Everybody, everybody,
everybody's had the blues.
One time or other everybody listen to me,
you lose somebody you love
But that's no reason for you to break down and cry

I said a hey, everybody, everybody,
everybody's had a lonely moment.
Everybody, everybody,
everybody's had the blues.
One time or other everybody listen to me,
you lose somebody you love.
That's no reason for you to break down
and cry.
I said a hey, everybody, everybody,
everybody's had a lonely moment.
Everybody, everybody,
everybody's had the blues.

Here he goes. And that's Tommy Rowe, of course, and that one's called Hey Everybody and that's instant survey number one for about the fourth day in a row.

Refreshing as a glass of water, that's the taste, fresh taste that Hamm's has captured. Rural Texas, the people of Hamm's say thank you. Yes, thanks for making Hamm's beer such a favorite. It's got that famous taste that thousands of Texans are enjoying every day. In fact, somewhere in Texas, someone is opening and enjoying a Hamm's beer every three seconds. This weekend is the perfect time to refresh yourself with a cold Hamm's beer. Thanks again for the spectacular welcome. May we suggest you stock up for the weekend with Texas brewed premium Hamm's beer at popular Texas prices. Refreshing as a glass of water, that's the taste, fresh taste of Hamm's.

Hey, be sure that you stock up for this weekend with Texas-brewed premium Hamm's beer at popular Texas prices.

And now we take you to KLIF Mobile Unit No. 4 in downtown Dallas.

The latest information—and things are rather confused at this moment—shots definitely were fired at the presidential motorcade as it passed through downtown Dallas. All squads are converging code three in the area of Elm and Houston in downtown. There is a tentative description of the shooting suspect. A man, a white male believed to be approximately thirty years old, reportedly armed with a thirty caliber rifle. How many shots were fired, how many persons, if any, were struck and wounded, we do not know yet. Very closed-mouthed officials are clamping down on the entire story. We'll bring you what details are available just as quickly as they come into our possession.

Sandra Dee has her troubles. Listen. A lot's been said about the wild teenage thing. But wait till you see the scrapes my dad Jimmy Stewart gets into. Yikes! You just wouldn't believe it. Can you picture Jimmy Stewart battling the police? Get 'em boy! Now! Oh no you don't! Mixed up with a French cutie. Holy Chihuahua! Doing a striptease. Yikes. You've just got to see our new picture, Take Her, She's Mine, to believe it. The wonderful Broadway smash is even funnier on the movie screen. Take Her, She's Mine, the hilarious story of a baby who suddenly becomes a babe. So take her, take him, take the family to see James Stewart and Sandra Dee in Take Her, She's Mine, co-starring Audrey Meadows. From Twentieth Century Fox in color by Deluxe. Take Her, She's Mine.

I'll do it friend, if you don't watch me very closely. It's the surprise fun show of the season now held over for a third big week at Interstate Palace Theater in Dallas.

You know that once upon a time
I didn't need you so
It would have been so easy then
For me to turn and go
But now there's no leavin' you
I know that for a fact

I'm at the point of no return
And for me there'll be no turning back
I told myself you'd always be
A habit I could break
But now a day without your kiss
Would be so hard to take
You just can't get off a train
That's movin' down the track
I'm at the point of no return
And for me there'll be no turning back
Once I could have said goodbye, but that was at the start
Now I think I'd rather die than be the one to say we'll part
Maybe you will break my heart
Or maybe you'll be true
No matter what the future brings
I've got to see it through
Maybe your love for me is nothin' but an act
I'm at the point of no return
And for me there'll be no turnin' back
Yeah, for me there'll be no turnin' back
Unh, unh, unh, unh, unh, unh

That's Gene McDaniels with a KLIF classic. And ladies and gentlemen stand by at 1190 on your dial for further developments in the reported shooting during the motorcade of President Kennedy on his visit to Dallas, Texas.

Are you hoping that someday you'll find something that's really good for pimples and a bad complexion? Search no more. Baker's Beauty Lotion is what you need. A brand-new, modern formula. Safe, easy, and pleasant to use. Mrs. H.W. Henchbeth, 1044 Garden View Drive, Dallas, says: My grandson had pimples all over his face and Baker's Beauty Lotion sure has done wonders for him. I highly recommend it for pimples and skin blemishes. Baker's

Beauty Lotion is a part of the old reliable Baker's Hair Tonic for dandruff. For pimples and bad complexion, Baker's Beauty Lotion is the best yet. It's a new formula containing no harmful or unpleasant ingredients. It's easy and safe to use. Those who use Baker's Beauty Lotion face the world with a clear face. Or your money back.

And now another report from downtown Dallas.

Details on the chase and search in downtown Dallas. An unidentified man fired several shots from what apparently was a high-powered thirty-thirty caliber rifle at the presidential motorcade. So far, the authorities are not releasing details on who, if anyone, was hit by any of the bullets or how badly they were injured. Parkland Hospital, being very closed now about the situation, but the search now centers at the area of Elm and Houston near the Old Texas Schoolbook Depository building and there is a possibility that the would-be assassin is still inside that building. All of the available downtown units are converging at emergency speed to that area. The entire area has been blocked off and is roped off now. No one allowed in or out as the search for this would-be presidential assassin continues in downtown Dallas. What has been a very smooth journey to Texas for the president and his, uh, wife and other officials, Vice President and Mrs. Lyndon Johnson, now has turned into another black smear. And we are keeping up to date on all the details through official police sources and we'll bring you full details as soon as they're available.

I do ninety percent of your work. I'm Bab-O cleanser. Grease dissolving, stain removing, powerful new Bab-O. Now do you believe me?

KLIF, 1190. Break in!

This is the KLIF newsroom. The police department is still trying to confirm the fact that President Kennedy and Governor John Connally have been wounded, perhaps tragically in a late-morning shooting in in the downtown area. According to the latest reports, both have been cut down by at least three bullets that pierced the atmosphere as the motorcade made its way from Love Field through the downtown area to the Trade Mart where President Kennedy was to speak at a luncheon. They were riding in an open automobile when the shots were fired. The bubble had been discarded when the sun broke through the clouds here in Big D. The president, his body cradled in the arms of Mrs. Kennedy, has been rushed to Parkland Hospital. We are still waiting word from Parkland the extent of his injury. We just talked with the police department just a moment ago. Here was the conversation.

Can you give us confirmation that the president has been shot?

No sir.

Can you give us the description again, please, ma'am?

Well, we're busy right now. Did you get it off the radio or, uh…? It's a white male, thirty-thirty caliber rifle and, uh, uh, I believe it's at Elm and Houston where it came from. Now, I don't know definitely and I don't like to say…

That was the police department, Mrs. Shrimpton saying they have not received a confirmed report. And now we'll switch you to the downtown area of Dallas and this is Joe Long.

This is the latest unconfirmed report we have—and we must stress that this is unconfirmed but it comes from a very high placed official who refuses to be quoted—it is now reported that Governor Connally and the president have perhaps been wounded in this assassin's attempt. It is an unofficial report that both the president and Governor Connally were wounded in this event of the shooting in the downtown area during the passing of the motorcade. The automobile in which the president was riding reportedly sped out to Parkland Hospital and, uh, we do not know if Mrs. Kennedy or Mrs. Connally suffered any injury. The first report we had said that both of the men were lying prone in the automobile, in the caravan limousine, at the time it made its way rapidly to Parkland Hospital. We have no further details. Parkland Hospital is being placed off-limits to reporters at this time but those details that are available will be brought to you just as quickly as we possibly can. Very briefly recapping, there has been an assassination attempt in downtown Dallas. Shots fired from a high powered rifle at the presidential car in the motorcade as it was en route to the Trade Mart for a scheduled presidential speech. All of the security precautions have been taken and now this happened. And, uh, the police are converging on and surrounding the area of Elm and Houston, the Old Technical Schoolbook Exchange building where they believe they may have trapped the would-be assassin. We'll bring you further details momentarily. Joe Long with Mobile Unit Number Four. 1190 and out.

We're back at the KLIF studios issuing the bulletin again for the man armed with the thirty-thirty caliber rifle. He was described as about five feet, ten inches, one-hundred-sixty-five pounds, a slender build, about thirty or thirty-five years old. This tragic incident occurred at Elm and Houston as the motorcade was en route to the Trade Mart for a noon luncheon. The president, of course, was to deliver a speech during his appearance in Big D. Newsmen, uh, some five car lengths behind the president heard what sounded like three bursts of gunfire. Secret Service agents in the auto following the president quickly pulled out automatic rifles. The bubble, as we'd mentioned previously, on the president's car was down when the shots rang out. The president slumped over the back seat, face down. Governor Connally lay on the floor of the rear seat. Wounds in the governor's chest were clearly visible. The wounds indicated that an automatic weapon had been used. Police say this is believed to be a thirty-thirty caliber pistol, er, rather rifle. Three loud bursts of gunfire, a possible tragedy on this November twenty-second in Big D. We're going to switch now to the Trade Mart and, uh, here is a statement from Gordon McLendon.

Gordon McLendon at the Trade Mart in Dallas. Here the scene is of wild pandemonium as two thousand guests waited anxiously for President Kennedy, Governor Connally, and the vice president. Now, rumors run rampant. No one here knows what has happened, but the rumors continue to circulate that the president and Governor Connally have both been shot. And, here at the Trade Mart, we have nothing but rumors and a wild scene of chaos. This is Gordon McLendon from the Trade Mart in Dallas.

That was Gordon McLendon from the Trade Mart in Dallas. Again, we are still trying to get confirmed reports from Parkland Hospital that President Kennedy and Governor Connally have been cut down by an assassin's bullet, a fusillade of bullets at the intersection of Elm and Houston in downtown Dallas. It is impossible—and it was impossible at that time—to tell where the president was hit, but bullet wounds in Connally's chest clearly indicated that he had been wounded in that region. There were three loud bursts visibly heard by members of the motorcade of the president, who quickly leaped off their bikes and raced up a grassy hill. That description again, a man about five feet, ten inches, one-hundred-sixty-five pounds, about thirty years of age, he was armed with a thirty-thirty caliber rifle. He was of slender build. The police department has thrown out an extensive dragnet. We are still trying to get in touch with Parkland Hospital, where we hope to have confirmation. The latest report that we have from one press source, Clint Hill, a Secret Service agent assigned to Mrs. Kennedy said, he's dead, as the president was lifted from rear of the White House touring car. Mr. Kennedy was rushed to the Parkland Hospital emergency room. Other White House officials reported that the hospital corridors erupted in pandemonium. The incident occurred at Elm and Houston in the downtown area as the motorcade wended its way through the region. Newsmen in the motorcade did hear the three bursts from the automatic rifle. It is impossible and was so at the time to tell where the Chief Executive was struck by the bullets. We are now in contact with, uh, one of our news units and we are going to switch you now for another report from the downtown section of Dallas.

Joe Long again from Mobile Unit No. 4. The police cordon and the wide search net continues. We still do not know whether this would-be assassin is trapped in the building or in the area at all. The search continues. We're going to vacate this mobile unit momentarily and we'll be back in touch with you just as quickly as possible. KLIF newsmen and mobile units are spread throughout the strategic spots, uh, covering this story. We'll bring you full details momentarily. Joe Long, Mobile Unit Number Four. 1190 and out.

The possible tragedy came after President Kennedy arrived three minutes late at Love Field as his big jet plane with number one on its side floated down to earth and the sun broke through the clouds. After the president was ten minutes away leaving Fort Worth, he was ten minutes late... he was three minutes late arriving at Dallas Love Field. An estimated two hundred fifty thousand persons lined the streets this afternoon as the president's motorcade moved through the streets. Then at twelve fifty p.m. Central time, acting White House news secretary Malcolm Kilduff was asked whether the president was dead. He said, I have no word now and that is the word we are awaiting. I have no word now, the latest. Congressman Jim Wright of Fort Worth had just said that both President Kennedy and Governor Connally were seriously wounded in the attack but were alive. This is the latest: Congressman Jim Wright of Fort Worth has said that both President Kennedy and Governor Connally were seriously wounded but were still alive and now here is KLIF's Joe Long.

Still no official word from Parkland Hospital. We were en route from Love Field. We had described the arrival of the presidential party and that is when the first word of the shooting came out. We have been in the deep downtown area in the area of Elm and Houston and the dragnet continues. So far Parkland Hospital has not released an official statement of President Kennedy and Governor John Connally. We do know now, however, that both of these men were wounded in the assassination attempt. And the dragnet and search continues. We are finding these details slow in coming. We have many official and unofficial comments coming from various sources, but at this moment, let's summarize it this way: As the presidential motorcade made its way through downtown Dallas, at least three shots rang out in the vicinity of Elm and Houston and one child reportedly was a witness to the shooting, uh, a young colored boy, who said that as he heard the first shot, he looked up at the fourth floor window of the Old Texas Schoolbook Exchange Building and saw a man leaning from the window and then he fired at least two more shots. The report we had from witnesses at the scene said that both the president and Governor Connally were lying prone in the presidential limousine as it had sped to Parkland Hospital. From Parkland, Congressman Jim Wright of Fort Worth said that both Kennedy and Connally were seriously wounded but are still alive. However we must stress that this is an unofficial report. It is not a medical report. Here is a description now, of the man who fired the shots.

Well, we're busy right now. Did you get it off the radio or, uh...? It's a white male, thirty-thirty caliber rifle and, uh, uh, I believe it's at Elm and Houston where it came from. Now, I don't know definitely and I don't like to say...

That was an official police department dispatcher description of the man we believe fired the would-be deadly shots at the presidential motorcade. There were about two hundred fifty thousand persons lining the downtown streets at the time this incident took place. As the motorcade made its way toward the triple underpass, the crowd would break up and flood into the streets. But still it was an orderly crowd, held back from the streets at the time the shooting occurred. Obviously this had to be a high-powered rifle for there to have been such a degree of accuracy on the part of the assassin firing bullets into both the president and Governor Connally. It was approximately twelve fifty our time when acting White House news secretary Malcolm Kilduff was asked whether the president was dead. He said I have no word at this time. That is acting news secretary Kilduff who made the trip instead of the usual White House news corps. Vice President Johnson was in the car behind the president and there was, uh, no indication at all that he was injured. Also, we do not have any indication whether the First Lady, Mrs. Jackie Kennedy or Mrs. John Connally suffered any injuries.

The report we have now, here it is, officially Mrs. Kennedy apparently is safe, Mrs. Connally also safe it appears to those witnesses at Parkland Hospital and, um, to say it mildly, both women extremely stunned. Mrs. Kennedy reportedly had cradled her husband's head in her lap during the speedy trip to Parkland Hospital. Kennedy, according to a member of his staff, was still alive ten minutes ago. Ten minutes ago we had word that the president was still alive. The blood was spattered all over the inside of the limousine, which had been flown in specially to carry the president. Ordinarily there is a huge plastic bubble which allows the public a view of the president and those in the car with him, but gives those inside the limousine protection from the weather and would-be assassins. But because of the rapid, beautiful turn in today's weather, the bubble had been removed and the president and all those in the limousine were fully exposed not only to the public and the elements, but also to these would-be killer bullets. Congressman Jim Wright of Fort Worth, as we told you earlier—he, in addition to Kilduff, would be perhaps the most official source we've been able to contact so far—told us that both Kennedy and Connally were seriously wounded, but as of twelve fifty-five, eleven minutes ago, both were alive. A call has been sent out for some of the top surgical specialists in the city. A call also has been placed for a priest to report to Parkland Hospital.

Now, let's summarize this so we can bring you up to date and give you full details of all the facts that we have available at our disposal at this moment. President Kennedy arrived in Dallas at approximately eleven thirty-five. He received a rousing welcome from some two thousand spectators at Dallas-Love Field. Then the motorcade began its trip through downtown Dallas to the Trade Mart, where he was scheduled to address some two thousand five hundred spectators and supporters. But just short of the moment he would have left the downtown area, as the motorcade began its trip toward the triple underpass at Elm and Houston, three bullets rang out, apparently fired from a thirty-thirty caliber rifle. The assassin supposedly was in a building about three or four stories up when he unleashed the deadly veil of bullets. We said deadly. That word was ill-advised. We will correct that. We do know, however, that the president and Governor Connally, both riding in the presidential limousine were wounded. As they departed Love Field, the president and Mrs. Kennedy sat on the main back seat and Governor Connally and his wife were on the jump seat. The Secret Service men and the chauffeur were in the front seat, but as witnesses stated, both men were prone in the vehicle. They did not bother with ambulances. The police escort made its way immediately to Parkland Hospital where top surgical specialists have been summoned. A call also has gone out for a priest. At this moment, word is that both men are still alive as of twelve fifty-five. The picture in downtown Dallas is one of extreme activity on the part of the police. There was that sudden call: all units report code three to the downtown area of Elm and Houston. They are trying to surround this building and close it off in case this man still would be there. He is approximately five feet, eight inches tall, weighs about one-hundred-sixty pounds, and is a white man. He was carrying a thirty-thirty caliber rifle. We're going to call Roy Nichols in one of the KLIF mobile units downtown to see what details he has on the search for the would-be killer.

We have just left the corner of Elm and Harwood where the shooting took place. There is no information to be gained at that point right now other than what Joe has just told you. Police are still looking for the would-be assassin. We will be at Parkland Hospital in just a moment to see if we can gain any information from Parkland at all.

Of course Parkland is not putting out any information at the moment as to whether the president and Governor Connally have been critically wounded or not. But we will be there in just a moment and will bring you the official word from Parkland Hospital as soon as it is released. At Elm and Harwood, of course, police have converged on the area, still searching for the would-be assassin. We'll be at Parkland in just a moment and we hope to have an official report as soon as we get there. Roy Nichols, Mobile Unit Number Four, out.

We now have received word from Parkland Hospital that the president is still alive. No official report yet on Governor Connally's condition, however, both men were alive at twelve fifty. We do now have information that both—or rather that President Kennedy—is still alive. Word from Hyannis Port Massachusetts, just handed to us. Word is that President Kennedy's mother and father have been advised that he has been shot here in Dallas. They are presently at Hyannis Port. And from New York City, only minutes after the president was shot, stocks moved actively lower, but a few issues stayed on the upside.

The search continues through downtown Dallas for the man who today loaded a gun and intended to snuff out the life of the president of the United States and the governor of the state of Texas, John Connally. How closely he has come to accomplishing his devious aim we do not know. We do have word that the president is still alive but the true extent of his injuries and what his present condition might be, we have not yet received official word on that. Top surgical specialists have been summoned to Parkland. A priest also has been summoned there. The president and Governor Connally, riding in the same car were rushed directly to Parkland Hospital as the motorcade broke up once this shooting incident took place. The first lady and Mrs.

Connally, neither of them suffered any injuries from the gunfire. That's the latest word we have on their condition but both women, of course, in a high degree of agitation and state of shock over the wounding of their husbands. It was reported to us by one bystander that as the vehicles sped toward Parkland Hospital, the first lady cradled the president's head in her lap. Governor Connally and the president were prone in the automobile. Having been past the intersection of Elm and Houston quite a number of times, if you will recall the Old Texas Textbook Exchange building, it sits only some twenty to thirty feet from the edge of the street where the presidential motorcade would have been passing. And from a three storey…third storey window, accuracy could be pretty well counted upon if a person knew how to use a weapon at all. Also, it would have been a very devastating shot, should it come into contact with the person for whom it was intended. So we still are awaiting more official word on how critically the president has been injured.

Everything seemed to be going well for Dallas today. The weather cleared up, everything cleared up, and the crowd was orderly at Love Field when the president arrived. It looked like Dallas was going to have a smoothly operating presidential motorcade and visit and speech and then departure this afternoon. And then suddenly, a black cloud descended on Dallas as the president and Governor Connally were wounded. We have only two official sources with whom we have been able to be in contact within the presidential party itself. Congressman Jim Wright of Fort Worth is one of those. He says that both the president and the governor have been seriously wounded but they are still alive. However, Clint Hill, a Secret Service agent assigned to protect Mrs. Kennedy had a much more critical description of the President's condition but, as we say, these are individual opinions and we have yet to receive direct official word from the surgeons at the hospital.

It is now reported to us by Parkland that president Kennedy is receiving blood transfusions. The president now receiving blood transfusions as a result of these assassin's bullets that tore into his body today. Three shots reportedly were fired at the motorcade.

And now we have word that a twenty-five-year-old man has been caught at Field and Elm Street. He obviously is a suspect in this assassination attempt. He has been captured at Field and Elm and is being taken directly to police headquarters. We will be in touch with our reporter at police headquarters to let you know precisely, how accurately this man might be fitting the description of the man for whom they've been searching ever since the shots were fired that struck the president and the governor. Although Dallas has been regarded as a stronghold of political opposition to Kennedy, the heavy street crowds between Love Field and the scene of the shooting were overwhelmingly friendly. They were friendly at Love Field. There were a few derogatory signs but there were no physical incidents of, uh, any note at all. There were numerous Welcome Kennedy signs, a few anti-Kennedy signs, but all in all, the crowd was very orderly...all but one person. And that person is the subject on the lips of the world at this moment, as he has pumped bullets into the body of President Kennedy and Governor John Connally, both of whom have been rushed to Parkland Hospital. Our reporters are in direct touch with the police department and Parkland Hospital. The search through the downtown area continues as we attempt to determine who has done this, has he been caught, and in what condition are we finding the president and Governor John Connally.

The latest word from Parkland Hospital is that the

president is receiving blood transfusions. He has been wounded, but he is alive. And the downtown area is not the place to be this moment unless you are on official business because the police department, the Secret Service, the highway patrol and the sheriff's office are making one of the biggest manhunts in all Texas—in fact all the nation— as they attempt to find the man who fired these shots at the president. One man perched on the roof of his car had held up to the president a sign saying that, because of Kennedy's socialistic beliefs quote, I hold you in complete contempt. That was one of the few derogatory signs that we have found in the downtown area. And now, back to Gary DeLaune.

The police have reported that they arrested a man about twenty-five years of age, fitting the description broadcast earlier by the Dallas Police Department, five feet, ten inches, one-hundred-sixty-five pounds. This last report stated that the president is undergoing emergency transfusions at this time at Parkland Hospital. The last word that we had shortly before one o'clock, about two minutes before one is that both the president and Governor John Connally were fighting for their lives. The man armed…believed armed with a thirty-thirty caliber rifle was perched from a building at Elm and Houston as the motorcade made its way to the Trade Mart. Now it is a very dejected, depressing, desolate room where the luncheon was to have taken place. A city in great apprehension this afternoon. The New York Stock Exchange closed operations after word of the assassination attempt against the president and Governor Connally. The Cotton and Wool Exchanges also closed. We are still awaiting word from Parkland Hospital as to the immediate condition of the president. As of sixteen minutes ago he was still battling for his life, undergoing blood transfusions. There have been, uh, many incidents in Big D in recent weeks that have tarnished the reputation of Dallas and this morning it appeared that the city in Texas we call The Gateway to the South was going to have a chance to redeem itself. The sun broke through the clouds and about two thousand persons gathered at the airport to greet the president. Departing from political procedures somewhat, the president left the limousine and walked behind the car. Mrs. Kennedy did likewise. They shook hands with well-wishers alongside the Love Field fence. Then the president and Mrs. Kennedy, Mr. and Mrs. Johnson, Governor and Mrs. Connally greeted their cars and made their way to the downtown area. At twenty minutes before one, approximately, the dastardly deed was done here in Dallas—that was the approximate time we received the news. One man was perched on the roof of his automobile. He held out toward the president a sign saying that because of Kennedy's socialistic beliefs, I hold you in complete contempt. And now we're going to turn you back over to Joe Long.

Let's summarize again precisely what has occurred here today. President Kennedy and his official traveling party took off from Fort Worth Carswell Air Base this morning shortly after eleven o'clock. He arrived in Dallas shortly past eleven thirty. Everything went smoothly. The rain cleared away, the sun came out, there was a good crowd on hand, well-behaved. The president departed from protocol. He left the official limousine, walked along the fenced area shaking hands with the spectators. Then the motorcade departed and the trip had just about concluded when the three shots rang out from an assassin's rifle, striking the president and Governor John Connally. Both men rushed to Dallas Parkland Hospital by emergency speed. Official surgical reports are not available at this moment. A special carton of blood, apparently for

transfusion purposes, has been rushed into the emergency ward. Two Dallas police officers carried that carton.
The president's body was limp as he was carried into the hospital, cradled in the arms of his wife. He was rushed to Parkland Hospital. The governor was also taken there. The surgical specialists have been called in. A Roman Catholic priest also has been sent for. Shortly after the shooting, Congressman Jim Wright of Fort Worth said both the president and Connally were alive, but seriously wounded.

And now here's a late report from Dallas police. One Secret Service agent reportedly was killed in the assassin's attempt. The Secret Service men have been in Dallas throughout the week, paving the way for this trip, hoping that it would go smoothly but, no, this has not been the case today. In fact, it has gone tragically at this moment. We now have reports that a twenty-five-year-old man has been arrested in the downtown area, a hot suspect in this case. The assassin apparently fired his shots from a thirty caliber rifle from a third floor window of a schoolbook exchange building, just before the presidential motorcade was to go under a triple-overpass, then out on to the main Stemmons Expressway, along to the Trade Mart, where the president was to have lunch and give his address. Blood was spattered all over the White House car. Mr. Kennedy was slumped over the back seat. Governor Connally lay on the floor at the rear of the seat. Mrs. Kennedy apparently was not hurt. Mrs. Connally was safe. The witnesses in the downtown area said there were three loud bursts of gunfire. The motorcycle police who were escorting the president quickly jumped from their bikes and raced up a grassy hill to take up position for possible action against the assassin. At the height of the emergency room drama, a weeping Negro woman bearing a small bloody child rushed into the hospital, where a nurse and intern went quickly to her side. The business of Parkland Hospital emergency room is continuous, twenty-four hours a day, but never has it been so busy with such a distinguished pair of patients as they have received there today—Governor John Connally and President Kennedy, both wounded in an assassination attempt in downtown Dallas. One man has been arrested as a prime suspect. He fits fairly closely the description of the man who supposedly fired these bullets. He was arrested in the vicinity of Elm and Houston where the dragnet has been for some forty-five minutes now and is being rushed to police headquarters for further questioning. There was absolutely no warning that this would take place. Of course these things always come so spontaneously. Should there be any warning, then the president would be better protected and an alternate route could have been prepared. But everything had gone smoothly to this very moment. Then, the three shots rang out and the vehicle bearing the president and the governor rushed to Parkland Hospital, both men prone in the back seat area of the vehicle. The president's head was cradled in the first lady's lap. We repeat—both Mrs. Kennedy and Mrs. Connally apparently escaped any injury from this assassination attempt. But it is now official, both President Kennedy and Governor Connally have been shot and wounded. At Parkland Hospital, top surgical specialists have arrived, a Roman Catholic priest has arrived, and a few moments ago, a special shipment of blood was brought in by two Dallas police officers. Bill Tomlinson, an assistant to Governor Connally talked from the operating room—this is late word from Parkland—saying that the governor had been shot just below the shoulder blade in the back. Tomlinson said he asked Connally how it happened and he said, I don't know, I guess from the back, but they got the president too. Congressman Jim Wright of Fort Worth says that both men were still alive as of twelve fifty-five Dallas time, approximately thirty minutes ago, but all indications—according to the extensiveness of the treatment at Parkland Hospital—every indication we have is that the wounds possibly are of a serious nature. The latest report from United Press International leads off this way: President Kennedy has been shot. He is perhaps fatally wounded. But we must keep repeating that there is no official word that the president is in critical condition at this time. However, he was slumped over in the back seat from the impact of the high caliber bullets that were poured into the back seat of the presidential limousine.

The last shooting incident involving a president occurred in 1950, when President Harry Truman was in office and living in Blair House in Washington when The White House was being renovated. Two Puerto Rican nationalists tried to gun their way into Blair House and assassinate Truman, who was taking a nap at the time on the second floor. One White House officer was killed in that assassination attempt and another was seriously wounded, and one of the assassins was cut down in the blaze of defensive gunfire on Pennsylvania Avenue. The Senate has adjourned in Washington upon learning of the assassination attempt. The American Stock Exchange closed its operations today after word of the attempt and the New York Stock Exchange took an expected dip.

Late word from Parkland Hospital. A Father Huber of Holy Trinity Church in Dallas has administered the last sacraments of the church to the president. This does not mean that the president has died. It is a religious precaution for those persons who are seriously ill or who have been seriously injured. But a Father Huber of the Holy Trinity Church of Dallas has at Parkland Hospital administered the last sacraments of the Roman Catholic Church to the president. There have been many reports coming from Parkland Hospital, some of which we have been able to confirm, others we have not. But we must stress this: KLIF is only accepting news from official sources, those with whom we are in contact with daily, those persons we know and can be absolutely certain of the reliability of their statements. So what you hear us broadcast, please bear in mind it is all of official nature or of eyewitness detail.

Sheriff's officers took a young man into custody at the scene. They are questioning him behind closed doors. But the word from Parkland is that a Roman Catholic priest has administered the last sacraments of the church to the president. The sacrament was administered shortly before one o'clock. However, we have received no further word on the severity of the president's condition. There are reports circulating by other news media in Dallas that the president has been killed, but we have yet to receive our official source word on this from Parkland Hospital or any of the other officials involved in this operation. A prime suspect in the assassination attempt is in custody. He is being questioned.

And now, we will see if Roy Nichols has made his way back into the mobile unit. He has been at Parkland Hospital and at the search scene. Perhaps we can contact Roy Nichols now. Roy obviously is out of the unit at Parkland Hospital checking with emergency sources there at this time. But at last report, the president and Governor Connally both have received transfusions. A Roman Catholic priest has administered last sacraments of the Church to the president. We do not know how seriously he was injured but Governor Connally was conscious in the hospital emergency room. One of his aides, Bill Stinson— he's an assistant to the governor—says that he talked to the governor in the hospital operating room and said the governor was shot just below the shoulder blade in the back. Stinson said he asked Connally how it happened and he said, I don't know, I guess from the back, but they got the president too.

So that's the situation to this moment as we await further official word on the condition of President Kennedy, who has been rushed to Parkland Hospital after being shot, bullets crashing from a high-powered rifle in the downtown Dallas area, almost at the conclusion of a near-perfect reception and motorcade from Dallas-Love Field. It was headed for the Trade Mart, where some two thousand five hundred supporters and well-wishers stood by waiting to greet the president and to hear the address he was to give there this afternoon. So that is the situation to this moment. One suspect is in custody. The last rites of the Church have been administered to the president. Another priest, who declined to give his name, said the Chief Executive still was alive at the time the sacrament was administered shortly before one o'clock Dallas time. Sheriff's officers have a young man—the prime suspect in custody at the scene—and are questioning him behind closed doors at this moment. The dragnet was all over all of the downtown Dallas area, but most of all, it was concentrated in the vicinity of Elm and Houston Streets, where the bullets were fired. The presidential car immediately sped the president and Governor Connally to Parkland Hospital. Emergency blood supplies have been brought in, top surgeons have been called in, and two priests—two Catholic priests who were summoned to the scene—one has administered the last sacrament of the Church to the president, but at last report, he apparently is still alive and how critical his injuries may be we have not yet been able to determine.

There is, uh, a strong rumor that the president is dead,

Joe, but until Parkland says it is official…but there is…is strong indication that the president of the United States is dead.

This is the strong indication. We have received several reports to that effect but as we have outlined before, until the official word is received, KLIF is withholding any stern and final pronouncement on that.

Were that true, Joe, it would be the second time in American history that a Johnson had seceded to the presidency from the death of a president, the last time having been, of course, the assassination of President Lincoln and he was, of course, seceded by Andrew Johnson. We have word that Vice President Lyndon Johnson is somewhere in Parkland Hospital. It has been impossible to determine his precise whereabouts at this moment. He was reported, of course, badly shocked by the shooting. Doctors were trying to keep him as quiet as possible. Vice President Johnson occupied the limousine directly behind the president's car. He is now under heavy Secret Service and police protection. Throughout the Texas trip, when Kennedy and Johnson had been in the same motorcade—as an obvious security measure—they have ridden in separate cars as they did today. The Johnson car has always been some distance behind the presidential car. Senator Ralph Yarborough, in a nearby car said he saw the president's lips moving at a normal rate of speed while he was being rushed to the hospital.

Gordon McLendon has just returned from the Trade Mart, where the scene that had been so beautifully set there for the president's arrival, the luncheon, and his speech this afternoon is empty now. Gordon, what was the effect on those, some two thousand people waiting there?

Stunned, of course, Joe. There was a wild scramble for transportation out of the Trade Mart, particularly by reporters from throughout the United States seeking to get transportation some way, somehow, to Parkland Hospital. By the time we left, which was approximately ten minutes after the shooting, the giant Trade Mart had been more than half-emptied of the two thousand people who had been assembled there to see the president, the vice president, and the remainder of the luminaries. Rumors ran rampant. At first it was, uh, thought that Vice President Johnson had also been shot in the attack. I can only say that no one at the Trade Mart knew very much, but now everyone is fully aware. Malcolm Kilduff, the acting press secretary—he is in charge of press relations on this tour—says he cannot say at this time whether the president is still alive and cannot say where he was hit. Says Kilduff, there are just too many stories at this time. Perhaps it was a gap in the motorcade, which we mentioned earlier, that saved Johnson from being a target today. These are the security precautions that they've been taking to keep the president and the vice president separated. The priest that accompanied Father Huber did not go into the emergency room itself. He said that he understood the president's condition was critical but was still alive at twelve fifty-five.

We're in direct contact, Joe, with Parkland Hospital. We are in direct contact. We have been unable yet to verify the rumors—and to this point they are strictly rumors—that the president is dead. We will not know until the word comes through officially, but there have been strong indications that the president has expired but, uh, again we repeat, it is unofficial. President Kennedy and Governor John Connally of Dallas, Texas having been cut down by assassin's bullets today at lunch. They were shot as they toured downtown Dallas in an open car. Specialists are arriving at the hospital—which I might mention is the scene of wild pandemonium. As we were coming from the

Trade Mart a moment ago in a Dallas police car, there was a call for twenty additional police units at Parkland Hospital. And, incidentally, on the fifth floor of the downtown building, from which the president and the governor were shot, they have now discovered empty rifle hulls and there is also indication that more than one man is involved in the attack. Joe?

We have had descriptions of three men, actually—two white men and one colored man—as being possible suspects in this shooting, but at present, a twenty-five-year-old white man has been taken into custody. He is behind heavy security guard at this time and is undergoing extensive questioning, but it obviously had to be a high-powered rifle in order to have the almost deadly effect it had from that distance. And it was just...you could say the motorcade was almost home free at the time this took place.

It was almost there.

It was leaving the most congested area of downtown. From there on, the route would have been relatively free of bystanders because it was a major expressway.

Clint Hill, a Secret Service agent assigned to Mrs. Kennedy, said as the president was lifted from the rear of the White Ho...House touring car at Parkland Hospital, he's dead. However, that again, comes under the category of an unconfirmed statement. We can only give you unconfirmed statements at this point. There are strong indications that the president has expired, but there has been no bulletin to that effect, and as Joe has told you, the last rites and sacrament has definitely been administered.

Correct. Two Catholic priests were summoned to the scene. Only one of them visited the president. That was the Father Huber and the word was that the president still was alive at the time the sacrament was administered, shortly before one o'clock Dallas time. Several of the surgeons have arrived. Blood plasma—a special carton of blood plasma—was brought into Parkland emergency not too long ago by two special Dallas police officers. Our KLIF reporters are in the downtown area where the search has been conducted for the would-be assassin, also at Parkland Hospital and at police headquarters and the sheriff's office to bring us the very latest and most official word that we are able to gather on this assassination attempt on the president's life today.

It would be the first time, of course, since the assassination of President McKinley that such an event has taken place in the United States and it would also be the second time in American history that a Johnson has seceded to the presidency upon the death of a president by assassination, the last time, of course, having been the secession of Andrew Johnson after the assassination of Abraham Lincoln. Joe?

At the time of these three shots—and that is a little confused right now as to how many there were, but we do know of three because that's the consensus of witnesses who were there—at the time the shots rang out, the motorcycle escort immediately jumped from their bikes, dashed up the grassy hill to the parkway just across the street from the Old Texas Schoolbook Exchange Building and began their perusal of the building. One policeman fell to the ground, pulled his pistol and screamed, get down. And a man across the street standing in the crowd snatched up his little girl and ran. This was the man the police first chased because he had panicked and run at the hearing of the shots.

The building, incidentally Joe, the correct name of that building—although it is the Texas Book Depository—is the Sexton Building. The Sexton Building.

Correct. And it is a very strategic point in the parade

route. Whoever pulled this devious act knew that he was choosing a key location for his attempt on the president's life.

Well of course the major attention is being focused on the condition of the president. No one yet has any authoritative report on the nature of the wounds to Governor Connally. Bullet wounds were plainly visible in Connally's chest, so we know that he was shot in the chest. His condition, however, remains more of a mystery that that of the President of the United States. The president is clearly gravely, critically, and perhaps fatally wounded. There are strong indications that he may already have expired although that is not official. We repeat, not official. But the extent of the injuries to Governor Connally is a closely shrouded secret at the moment.

President Kennedy is dead, Gordon. This is official word. The president is dead. The president, ladies and gentlemen, is dead at Parkland Hospital in Dallas.

The shock, uh, of an incident like this, particularly to those of us of the press, radio, and television corps, who had seen the president alive only a few moments ago, uh, can never be described. At Dallas-Love Field he arrived. He was his usual smiling self. He even deviated from protocol and went to the fence and shook hands with the people. So did Mrs. Kennedy. So did Vice President and Mrs. Johnson. And then the motorcade began its trip and then rang out the deadly bullets from the assassin's gun.

Ladies and gentlemen, the president of the United States is dead. The new president of the United States, by secession, is Lyndon Johnson. It will be the second time in American history that a Johnson has seceded to the presidency upon the assassination of the president. The last time being of course, uh, in the post-Civil War days upon the assassination of Abraham Lincoln, when Andrew Johnson seceded as president. And you will recall that this is the second assassination of this century, the last having been the assassination of William McKinley in 1901. President Kennedy and Governor John Connally of Texas, cut down by assassin's bullets, the condition yet of Connally undetermined. We know he's been shot in the chest. We do not know whether he has been shot once or twice, but bullet wounds were clearly visible in his chest. We repeat, ladies and gentlemen, the flash of a moment ago—and you get these flashes once in a lifetime—the president of the United States is dead.

Robert F. Kennedy

I.

My thanks to all of you and it's on to Chicago and let's win there.

We want Bobby! We want Bobby! We want Bobby! We want Bobby!

Senator. How are you going to counter Mr. Humphrey in his, uh, backgrounding you as far as the delegate votes go?

Senator Kennedy has been...Senator Kennedy has been shot! Is that possible? Is that possible? It could... Is it possible, ladies and gentlemen? It is possible he has... not only Senator Kennedy... Oh my God! Senator Kennedy has been shot. And another man, a Kennedy campaign manager. And possibly shot in the head. I am right here. Rafer Johnson has a hold of a man who apparently has fired the shot. He has fired the shot. He still has the gun. The gun is pointed at me right at this moment. I hope they can get the gun out of his hand. Be very careful. Get that gun! Get the gun! Get the gun! Stay away from the gun!

Get the gun!

Stay away from the gun! His hand is frozen. Get his

thumb! Get his thumb! Get his thumb! Take a hold of his thumb and break it if you have to! Get his thumb! Get away from the barrel! Get away from the barrel, man!

Watch it with the gun. Watch it with the gun!

Look out for the gun! Okay. Alright. That's it, Rafer! Get it! Get the gun, Rafer!

Get the gun! Get the gun!

Okay now hold onto the guy!

Get the gun! Get the gun!

Hold on to him! Hold on to him! Ladies and gentlemen, they have the gun away from the man. They've got the gun. I can't see…I can't see the man. I can't see who it is. Senator Kennedy, right now, is on the ground. He has been shot. This is a…this is… What is he? Wait a minute. Hold him! Hold him! Hold him! We don't want another Oswald! Hold him Rafer, we don't want another Oswald! Hold him, Rafer! Keep people away from him! Keep people away from him! Alright ladies and gentlemen, this is…now… Make room! Make room! Make room! Make room! Make room! The senator is on the ground. He's bleeding profusely…from apparently… Clear back!… Apparently the senator has been shot from the, ah, in the… frontal area. We can't see exactly where the…where the senator has been shot, but… C'mon. Push back. C'mon. Grab a hold of me. Grab a hold of me and let's let's pull back. That's it. C'mon. Get a hold of my arms. Let's pull back. Let's pull back. Alright. The senator is now… The ambulance has been called and the ambulance is… Bring the ambulance in this entrance! And…this is a terrible thing. It's reminiscent of the Valley the other day when the senator was out there and somebody hit him in the head with rock and people couldn't believe it at that time, but it is a fact. Keep room! Ethel Kennedy is standing by. She is calm. She is raising her hand high to motion people back. She's attempting to get calm. A woman…with a tremendous amount of presence. A tremendous amount of presence. It's impossible to believe. It's impossible to believe this. There's a…certain amount of fanaticism here now as this has occurred. No one… They're trying to run everybody back. Clear the area! Clear the area! Right at this moment…the senator apparently…we can't see if he is still conscious or not. Can you see if he is conscious?

What?

Can you see if he is conscious?

I don't know. He is half-conscious.

He is half-conscious. And ladies…we can't see, ladies and gentlemen. One of the men, a Kennedy, apparently a Kennedy supporter is going first… C'mon. Out! Out! Out! Is there some way to close these doors? Is there any doors here?

Get out! Get out!

Out through the…out through the exit. Let's go. Out we go.

Out.

Unbelievable situation. They're clearing the halls. One man has blood on himself. We're walking down the corridors here. Repetition in my speech. I have no alternative. The shock is is so great. My mouth is dry. I can only say that here in the kitchen of the Ambassador Hotel, the back entrance, from the podium, in the press room, the senator walked out the back. I was directly behind him. You heard a balloon go off and a shot. You didn't really realize that the shot was a shot. And yet a scream went up. Two men were on the ground, both bleeding profusely. One of them was Senator Robert Kennedy. At this moment, we are stunned, we are shaking, as is everyone else in this kitchen corridor at the Ambassador Hotel in Los Angeles. They're blocking off the entrance now, supposedly to make room for the ambulance. That's all we can report at this moment. I do not know if the senator is dead or if he is alive. We do not know the name of the other gentleman concerned. This is Andrew West, Mutual News, Los Angeles.

II.

...about three hundred fifty. David Hayward with two hundred sixty and Walter Tucker with two hundred thirty-five. For the Republicans in the Seventeenth, Richard Howard has about three hundred votes. In the Twenty-second, uh, congressional district, James Corman, incumbent, is having no trouble at this point with his reelection bid in the primary in any event. He has about eighty-four percent of the vote. The leader for the Republicans is Joe Holt with about fifty-five percent of the vote. In the Twenty-ninth congressional district, in...

Jerry I'm sorry we're going to have to interrupt you. We have to go to Ray Williams right now to Kennedy headquarters in the Ambassador Hotel.

Right, Bob, and here we have a situation. Senator Robert Kennedy has been shot. The man is now calling for a doctor.

Is there a doctor in the house?

We don't know exactly who did the shooting or how it happened. The rumor we have is that, in the midst of some hysterical teenagers, a shot rang out. There was a noise. No one knew at the time whether it was a balloon or just what, but the senator has been shot. Exactly what his condition is, we don't really know. However, our producer has gone over to check and see if he can find out anything, but there is complete pandemonium here at the Embassy

Room at the Ambassador Hotel. Women are hysterical, they have been screaming.

The best thing that anyone can do here...

No one really knows who did it, whether they have apprehended the person who shot him or what.

...is to leave the room in an orderly way.

They're now asking for everyone to leave the room in an orderly fashion. Perhaps once they clear this room, then we can begin to probe into this drastic incident that is taking place here, find out exactly what it is.

We don't know what has happened.

Right now the gentlemen in charge of the Kennedy party are trying very hard to retain their composure, hoping that this will affect the crowd and help them to move out in an orderly fashion.

Would you please clear the room? Would you please clear the room in an orderly fashion?

Bob, it's unbelievable, what has happened here at the Embassy Room. We now have our producer coming this way with a youngster who evidently was very close to what was going on. We should be able to find something from him. Bring him over here.

Please leave the room.

What happened?

I saw this man go in the back. He started running back. And I saw and I heard he's been shot. That's all I heard.

What, uh, what man was it?

It was young...it was a young person. That's all I saw. Run back... I saw...I just saw somebody run back and then I heard somebody say he's been shot. And that's all I heard.

There were two people that ran back.

That's all. I saw this man run back there.

There has...has been a chase after that man?

Well, everybody started…
Nobody said anything…
Nobody said anything.
…and then a bunch of people who ran out said he's been shot…he's been shot. I saw this man run in. Everybody started running after him and said, he's been shot and that's… Oh!

Did you hear him shot?

I heard…just, like, it was…like a balloon pop…a balloon pop…it was a muffled sound. That's all I heard when I was back there. I was going back there but they threw me back inside.

That was actually somewhat of an eyewitness report as to what has taken place here at the Embassy Room. This young man is completely exhausted. Evidently he was tossed around pretty good by those around the senator. We're going to switch back to you, Bob, and we ourselves are going down into this crowd and see if we can find out any more.

That was Ray Williams giving a very graphic description of a tragedy that's occurred on this night of the election, the Democratic presidential election. We say tragedy in the sense that Senator Kennedy has been shot. As Ray pointed out, he has no knowledge as to the extent of the injury or the extent of the wound, only that eyewitnesses said the senator had been shot. As you heard, uh, it is pandemonium. Officials there are trying to clear the room so that they can ascertain exactly what did happen or what did not happen. All we can go on at this time is the report that Ray has and, as you heard, it was fragmentary, as it must necessarily be in the scene of such confusion and such drama. So we will be standing by here.

It would be strange if, indeed, to have this California election primary—which has been filled with a great deal of drama and a great deal of excitement from the time that it started—to culminate in a disaster, meaning the expiration of the senator. We have no idea how seriously he has been wounded. We hesitate… We hasten to assure you that we will bring you that information just as soon as it's possible. Boyd?

Well, Bob, you said the word disaster and whether it was only a flesh wound, it's still a disaster to think that such a thing could happen in a crowded hotel room surrounded, as he undoubtedly would be, by admirers and by aides. How could such a thing happen? One just wonders how much tragedy one family can stand, the Kennedy family. Now let's go back to the Kennedy headquarters and Ray Williams.

Boyd, we have here our own Ray McMackin who was right there and he's going to fill us in exactly on what happened. Ray?

Boyd, I am sorry, but I can't hold back the tears. He's been shot right in the head. And he's not moving. There are several people back there who have also been shot, one right in the head. Excuse me… I just can't control it… He's not moving. His eyes are not open…and he's shot right in the head. He's laying on his back and there's two other people wounded, just bystanders. And I can't understand it… I was right there and it just… The doctors… It's just mass confusion. It's terrible.

And there you have it, a reporter that was standing right next to the incident, an eyewitness report.

Ray? Ray? This is…

A disaster has occurred here at the Embassy Room.

Ray? This is is Bob Arthur. Ray? Happiness has now turned into tragedy. The men on the stage are requesting more doctors. If what Ray says is true—and we have no cause to doubt his word—Senator Kennedy has suffered a severe head wound. Bob, I'm going to switch back to you and see if we can find out anymore as to what's going on.

And there is another chapter in this drama that's unfolding. As you can tell, Ray McMackin, KNX reporter overcome by emotion as he tried to report on what he had seen. From what we can gather, Senator McCarthy has been shot.

Senator Kennedy.

Senator Kennedy, I beg your pardon, yes. Senator Kennedy has been shot. It is a head wound as we understand and Ray McMackin said two other persons had…bystanders have also been wounded in the shooting. At this time we have no information as to who might have committed this crime, other than the fact that a man had been seen running from the scene. We're standing by waiting for Ray to return to the microphone. He's trying to investigate, to make a determination as to exactly what did happen to get as much information as possible so that he can relay it on to you.

Bob, from, uh, what Ray McMackin said, with two others wounded, apparently there would have to be more than one shot fired. And the first fragmentary reports that we got from Ray Williams said was that it sounded like a balloon popping. And that would lead us to believe that only one shot had been fired. Now it appears that more than one shot was fired. Do you have something from the wire services there?

Yes, but this is one of those things that usually adds to the confusion in something like this. Ray McMackin was there and said that the senator had been shot in the head. The Associated Press is saying that he was shot in the hip as he left the platform from which he made his victory statement. We are going to switch back right now to the Ambassador, where the PA system is operative enough to pick up the announcements as they are being made. It may be slightly chaotic, it may not be all connected, but you at least will be at the scene and then you will hear what we hear as it develops.

…mortally wounded and who are back in, uh, the anteroom now. There are at least three doctors there, two of whom were out here in the auditorium, the victory celebration room, listening to the Kennedy statement. Just a few minutes ago.

Everybody, please move out of here.

Take it easy…

This is Jerry Dunphy back at KNX election headquarters. We do have a little more definite information. Many people are reluctant to talk to the reporters on the scene. Senator Robert Kennedy was shot in the hip tonight in Los Angeles as he left the platform on which he made a victory statement, the statement you saw just about seven minutes ago. The scene at the Ambassador Hotel right now is one of shock and terror, really. Many shots were fired, as you heard. Senator Kennedy, brother of the assassinated President John Kennedy, lay on the floor of the hotel kitchen. Blood streamed over his face, his eyes were unseeing. That's the report that we have.

We are informed that the senator's assailant, as yet unidentified, has been…or is being held a few feet away by a half dozen of the Kennedy supporters.

Bob Ferris is outside the lobby on the telephone line. He has more information. Bob, come in.

Yes, we just saw a tremendous amount of people come out of the Embassy Room, actually. There were three or four policemen who had a young Negro person. They had their shotguns drawn, and were trying, uh, to get him out out of the hotel. I do not know whether he was a suspect or not, but apparently he was. The crowd

at least thought that he was and closed in on the police.
There were several fistfights that broke out here in the
lobby and finally, police and firemen shunted away the
crowd, which was eager to get at this, suspect—if it was a
suspect—and he was carried down the stairs and actually
out of the hotel. So, at this point, it appears that one of
the suspects—I can only say that it appears that one of
the suspects is a young Negro youth who was cringing
in the midst of this cordon of policemen with sawed-off
shotguns—was finally carried down the stairs and out of
the hotel. There is pandemonium in the lobby out here.
People are crying openly, weeping, and people are saying,
oh no, oh no. And there are fistfights around as various
people just plain get too emotional and attack each other.
This is Bob Ferris now in the Ambassador Hotel lobby. I'll
go out and see if I can find out what is happening now.
Back to you Bob Arthur at KNX news headquarters.

Thank you Bob. We're going to go back inside the
Ambassador now to Ray McMackin, an eyewitness. Ray,
come in.

Bob, Ray McMackin is right here next to me. We do
know that one lady who has suffered a head wound is
being treated here in the Embassy Room. Again, they're
asking the press and everyone else to back up so that they
can turn off some of the lights. The lights make it awful
hot. Here's Ray now, more composed, to give us more of
what he saw. Ray?

It was, uh, well, I'm a little more composed. I was
right there. I hope I never see a sight like that again. Ah,
this won't be a newsman's type of report, it will be quite
biased. It was terrible. Absolutely horrible. There was a man
wounded in his side, a young boy. I...I before I cracked up
here I...I...I had time to interview him. He was not severely
wounded. Right on the left side, uh, the right side of his hip

just above the, uh, bone there, and he's...he's alright. There was another man that was shot right in the stomach. He had blood all over his white shirt, from his chin all over the floor and he looked in bad shape. There was a woman that was shot right in the forehead, right smack in the forehead. When I saw Senator Kennedy, he was laying on the... After he fell... There was just, uh...it was just terrible... He was laying there... It was just, all over again, uh, the Dallas thing. Er, his, uh, eyes were closed, he was not moving. It took, uh, two, or three minutes to get a doctor. It seemed like hours, but they finally got a doctor in there and then they partitioned it off and all the newsmen were trying to back people off. It was mass confusion. I'll try to describe Senator Kennedy, but I'll never forget that sight as long as I live. He was lying there just... just... I hate to say it, but he was just dead still. His eyes were closed and there was blood, blood, blood all over the side of his head.

Ray's description, Bob, of exactly what he saw. As we said, in addition to treating this woman for her head wound, they are also searching suspects. Now, I would imagine that no one is going to be allowed to completely leave this hotel. I would imagine that it's completely sealed off at this particular time. Perhaps some of our men on the outside can give us more information on that. Bob, back to you now.

Ray Williams at the Kennedy headquarters in the Ambassador Hotel. Now we switch over to our sister station KNXT. Another eyewitness report.

...had some medical attention at that point?

No. I...no. I really I couldn't.

Was there...did he appear to be conscious?

No. He didn't appear to be conscious, no. He might have been...

He was conscious and coherent. I gave him a pair of

rosary beads, which are from Ireland. I told him and he looked straight up. I was wondering what this meant. I got a little frightened to see him looking straight up but, he looked at me. I said the act of contrition. I am a Roman Catholic. A Roman Catholic is trained to do this in case of any serious accident. I said to the president the act of contrition slowly and audibly and he heard it, I'm sure of it. He was breathing, he was alive. Please God. And I said to him, Mary, queen of peace, pray for us and with that he took my hand in the rosary beads and tightened.

Where was this, at what stage?

This was right after he was shot. I heard a balloon pop and I said to some woman, what a terrible thing to have around here. These…these sounds, I said, it's not good for another Kennedy. And the woman said, don't be silly. And that's when I realized it wasn't a balloon.

Was he…was he conscious when you left him?

He was conscious. I was pushed away from him. I didn't need to do…do any thinking about his consciousness. I did what I believe I could do…

Did you see where he was wounded, if he was wounded?

He was wounded. The blood came from his hand and from his ear. I believe he was shot in the rear of the neck. I'm not sure. His blood came…

Are you certain that it was the senator? Are you certain that it was the senator?

It was Senator Kennedy.

You definitely saw that?

I know it was Senator Kennedy.

Did you see anyone else shot?

I saw someone else.

Who was it? Do you know?

Was there a woman shot?

Did they get the suspect?

There was someone else shot. I did not look at…because I looked to see Senator Kennedy.

What did the person look like? Was it a man or woman who shot him?

I really cannot tell you. I…I didn't…I didn't take notice. I was looking for the senator. I'm a Catholic, uh…a little slightly moody, I guess.

Do you know how many people were shot?

I don't think more than two were shot. I don't know about the one who did the shooting. All I know I…they had him up on some bins, some towel bins.

It was a him? It was a he, right?

I saw curly hair. Yes and it was a male.

Was it a male, curly hair?

I don't know about any woman.

Was it blond hair? Black hair?

Hey, I don't…I just did what I could do. Thank you.

I've spoken…I've spoken to several eyewitnesses…

This is Jerry Dunphy back at KNX, the election headquarters. We have this late report. If you're finding it hard to see your television pictures at home, it's because the lights have gone out in the Embassy Ballroom at The Ambassador Hotel. The Kennedy campaign managers have asked reporters to leave and dim their television lights. When they wouldn't leave, they turned the lights out in the ballroom, just after Senator Kennedy was shot. We also have this note. An ambulance from Central Receiving Hospital was sent to the Ambassador Hotel to remove Senator Kennedy. That's all we know at this time. We don't know exactly where the senator was shot, whether it was the head, whether it was hip, how many people were shot, we don't have that, or how seriously injured the woman who was shot was hurt.

This is Bob Arthur at KNX election headquarters. Ray McMackin, KNX radio newsman, was on the scene, an eyewitness. And you heard his very emotional report a few moments ago. Ray, as an eyewitness, said at least three persons were shot—one shot in the arm, another shot in the stomach, and that still another had been shot...

...A young man, yes...he said was shot in the hip and a woman shot in the head. So that would be, uh, four altogether.

Yes, we're trying to piece all these things together.

Even as emotional as Ray McMackin was, I would tend to put more credence in his report than in the report that we just heard, which was the interview on television that four persons actually have been wounded. Whether or not any have expired, that will have to await further developments.

We do know, as Jerry Dunphy just said, that the senator is being rushed to Good Samaritan Hospital. John D. O'Connell, KNX radio newsman, is right behind the ambulance, and he will give us a report just as soon as he possibly can from the scene. We have a report added to this—Kennedy's brother-in-law, Stephen Smith, was one of those that was reportedly shot. The gunman, according to one report, was said to have been captured by Rafer Johnson, former Olympic decathlon champion and a Kennedy aide. This tragedy occurred right at a moment of triumph for Senator Kennedy—at least an appearance of triumph—because it has been pretty well established by the major news reporting services, including CBS and NBC, that Senator Kennedy had won the Democratic presidential nomination here in the California area, with something like fifty percent of the vote to McCarthy's thirty-nine percent. We are more or less flying as blind as you are on the subject because, as you have heard, the reports have been anything but complete. Probably the most complete report is that of Ray McMackin, our reporter, who was an eyewitness, but there is still some confusion in the minds of a great many people. To recap, Senator Kennedy was stepping from the platform, had just made what had appeared to be a victory statement thanking a great many individuals who had helped in his campaign, including Rafer Johnson, who had reportedly captured the gunman. And as he started to leave, he was shot along with at least three—possibly four—other persons. Bob Ferris, reporting from outside the Ambassador Hotel, said that heavily armed police had rushed a young man—and his report said a young Negro man—from the scene, apparently with the idea of getting him away as possibly could. Now we switch to John D. O'Connell on the mobile unit and here is his report.

Right Bob. The news bad at this hour. I've just pulled up behind the ambulance at Central Receiving Hospital. Senator Kennedy has been brought in on the stretcher here at Central Receiving Hospital. About sixteen police cruisers are also on hand here. The streets are now being roped off. I do hope everyone in the audience who can hear my voice will not come over here. It will only harm, rather than do any good. Senator Robert Kennedy is here at Central Receiving Hospital. He's been rushed into the emergency room. I'll report more as the news develops. This is John D. O'Connell at Central Receiving Hospital for KNX radio news.

John D. O'Connell on the scene and, as he said, he will relay to us whenever new information becomes avaiable. This much we do know, recapping again, because we're going from fragmentary reports—Senator Kennedy, brother of the assassinated president John F. Kennedy, was shot in the Ambassador Hotel, lying on the floor of the hotel kitchen after the shooting, blood streaming over his face, his eyes reportedly opened but unseeing. The Senator's assailant, as yet unidentified, apparently was captured by Rafer Johnson and a half dozen of Kennedy's supporters. Police reportedly, heavily armed, have rushed the young man or the suspect away from that scene apparently for interrogation. Boyd?

Bob, a thought just struck me. One of the last remarks that Senator Kennedy made, when he was making what appeared to be a victory statement, was a joking remark that he had received a message from his old adversary Mayor Sam Yorty that he had stayed too long. And little did anyone know at that moment that he had indeed stayed too long. I'm wondering if Ray McMackin has been able to compose himself, and whether we can reach him down at Kennedy headquarters, or whether or not we have been, uh...

I'm signaled that we cannot at this moment Boyd.

I would imagine that one of the first things they would try to do would be to move all of the news people out of there, and as we heard from Jerry Dunphy, they shut off the power so that the TV crews didn't have any lights anymore, removing some of the carnival atmosphere. Unfortunately, that's what always appears to be happening when all of the bright lights are on. Now we can go back to Kennedy headquarters. Here's Ray Williams.

Right Boyd. What's happening now is that evidently we're going to be ushered out of here very shortly. They want this room completely empty. They are now asking the television crews to remove their equipment, to conduct their interviews on the outside. No new evidence has come our way as to just what occurred or who was involved. All persons evidently involved in the shooting—those being shot as well as the suspects being apprehended—have been removed from the premises. The whole room is going to be cordoned off. Outside in the halls, we know it's complete bedlam. We understand that they've completely blocked off this building. The police are coming through now and they're making motions that it's going to be time for us to go.

Well, there was a request for another doctor, so we might still have one of the injured persons on the inside yet. But the big problem is that some of the Kennedy workers are still here. They're causing more confusion than the press. Members of the press are running around taking, in some instances, rampant reports that have no credence whatsoever, but that's the way it goes in a moment of tragedy like this. That's about the scene here at the Embassy Room—much quieter, much sadder, quite a bit more tragic that it was just an hour ago. Back to you, Bob.

Ray Williams there. We have added information and it's fragmentary, of course, that the apparent assailant, a man about 25 years of age, curly-haired and, according to this report, of Latin appearance, was captured by Kennedy supporters. He was rushed through The Ambassador Hotel lobby by police. If we dovetailed these reports, this will coincide and correlate with what Bob Ferris was saying from the outside. He had watched the armed police come rushing out with a suspect apparently in custody, and at that time, there was a number of fights that also broke out as people became excited and as rumors spread, as they always do in a case of this nature. Unfortunately, no one seems to have a clear and concise idea as to who the individual might be. We earlier had a report that it was Negro. Now it is of Latin American extraction, and we would hope that all would bear with us until we can sift out this fragmentary information and try to bring you a complete and accurate report as we possibly can. Ray

McMackin was an eyewitness to it. He said the senator had been shot and he said in the head. Three other persons have also been shot—we had a report that one was Kennedy's brother-in-law, Stephen Smith, another a woman, another a small child.

Bob, the thought occurs that something like this very definitely had to be premeditated. Someone with hate in his heart had to have thought to himself that this was what he wanted to do. He had to arm himself undoubtedly with a revolver, something that would be easily hidden. We'll now go to Senator McCarthy's headquarters.

Bob, I am witnessing a silent procession from the grand ballroom of McCarthy headquarters here at the Beverly Hills Hilton. The senator just sent down word about a minute and a half ago. He asked for a moment of silent prayer for Senator Robert Kennedy. There were probably about one hundred fifty still left in the grand ballroom. That wish was acknowledged. The moment of silent prayer ended just a few seconds ago and the senator asked that each, in his own way, then go home and meditate and say a few more silent prayers for Senator Robert Kennedy. So far, those are the only comments from Senator McCarthy. The grand ballroom here at the Beverly Hilton is very quiet, it is very solemn, it is subdued. That moment of silent prayer has been extended into several moments, not only for the supporters of Senator McCarthy, but for the newsmen from all of the broadcast media. This is Dennis Bracken from the grand ballroom, McCarthy headquarters. Back to Bob Arthur at KNX election headquarters.

The shooting of Senator Kennedy occurred right after he had spoken to about 1000 supporters in that crowded ballroom. His wife Ethel, who was with him was not injured.

Ray, you were pointing out a minute ago that someone had to premeditate this action.

Yes. Someone had to have hate in their heart and arm themselves with a weapon that could easily be hidden so they could get into this place and someone also had to figure out where the senator would be so he could interest intercept him. Someone very definitely planned this, someone with hate in their heart.

We would point out that that Senator Kennedy's appearances had been delayed throughout the course of the evening. As we know, he had been expected from almost ten o'clock on, but had delayed his appearance in The Ambassador Hotel so that he could watch the returns, and listen to the returns as they were broadcast checking, obviously, with his lieutenants up and down the coast to make some sort of determination as to whether or not he was, in fact, the winner of the California Democratic primary. When he became convinced in his own mind that he had won, then he did make that appearance. So, whoever did lie in wait for the senator apparently had been there for quite a long period of time, knowing the senator would eventually make some sort of an appearance and some sort of a statement, whether in victory or in defeat.

We have late information that has just been handed us. We had not yet been able to make contact with Central Receiving Hospital. The phone was finally answered after a great many tries but only silence followed, then taking that phone off the hook. We do know that John D. O'Connell of KNX news radio is at the hospital and just as soon as it possible for him to give us some information, he will.

Don Schulman, a witness, said that Senator Kennedy was walking to the kitchen when he was shot—and here's another report—three times by the gunman who stepped out of the crowd. We do know there was were a flurry of shots fired, and we that know others were also wounded. Shulman, who witnessed the shooting, said the gunman was shot by Kennedy bodyguards and taken into custody. This is in conflict with other statements that we've had. This we have found, in our experience as a newsmen, is the thing that normally happens in such a tragedy like this or when there are rapid-fire events taking place. A great many witness have a great many ideas and it takes some time in order for the true reports to come out. We had this recently in the case of Dr. Martin Luther King, who was shot fatally in Memphis. At that time, first reports had Dr. King being shot and wounded as he sat in a car outside the hotel, then later on shot on the balcony. As it turns out, that was the correct report.

Well, even more recently, Bob, when the senator was here on a campaign tour, he had made several stops and several appearances. And after a rally out in The Valley, when he was returning to his hotel, there were all sorts of reports that the senator had been hit with some sort of a missile or some such thing. I asked the senator himself about it at that time. He said nothing had happened. I got it then from another reporter who said that what had happened was that some youngsters standing on an overpass had wanted to drop some candy into the senator's car as he went by. The candy fell. Some of it apparently touched the senator. He was shocked and he sat down. And this led to all kinds of reports that the senator had been hit by a missile, he was hit in the head, he was hurt, and so on and so forth. So we do in these instances, have all sorts of conflicting reports. I say again Ray McMackin—a trained reporter on the scene there— should very well have given us a true picture of what is going on. Now we'll go back to Kennedy headquarters at the Ambassador Hotel. Ray? Is Ray McMackin there? Or Ray Williams? At the Ambassador Hotel?

We were expecting... Apparently they are not making

contact right now. We'll stand by and complete that call just as soon as we possibly can.

It would seem, as a result of this tragedy and other tragedies that have taken place in the last few years, that there will be greater and tighter security for the nation's major political candidates, no matter what the occasion, Boyd. There are many who have called for greater security in times past. Of course a candidate's appeal is that of being able to mingle with the crowd, to say hello, to shake hands, and to speak a few words. This, of course, puts him—under these trying circumstances—puts him in grave danger, as we know here. Of course, who would think for a moment that a victory celebration, such as the one that the senator was enjoying, that this would turn into a personal tragedy and personal injury to him? How you could possibly screen everyone at a victory celebration is the unanswered question. Obviously, you could not, unless candidates appearances are confined, away from large crowds and into appearances on television or appearances on radio. This again, takes the senator or the candidate— whoever he might be—out of that personal contact with the people. You must have contact in order to influence a voter and influence those who would cast their ballots. Now we're going to swing back to Kennedy headquarters to Ray Williams.

Well, Bob, my producer Marshall Boyd has been out in the crowd all evening getting people to interview. Just as Kennedy was leaving the platform, there was quite a bit of pandemonium that broke out. He immediately ran over to see what was happening as the females there were hysterically screaming. And he came back with the word that there had been a shooting. Now, he has talked with a friend of his and he will now tell us exactly what it was his friend related to him in connection with this tragedy.

Yes Ray, I saw a fireman friend of mine who wanted to remain anonymous, and he confirmed that Kennedy had been shot, that he had been taken to Central Receiving Hospital. He said the suspect was apprehended and that Kennedy fans and Kennedy supporters literally tried to beat the suspect to death—they were really giving him quite a pummeling on the ground.

Well, this was somewhat evident at the time that you ran over, that there was at least a fight in progress or some unnecessary commotion.

As you know, Ray, I went over there on a wild thousand-to-one shot trying to get Kennedy to go on microphone, and I heard screaming, which I thought were Beatle-type screams from young fans and I heard breaking glass and…and then people crying and saying that he had been shot…he had been shot and…

From that point on, Bob, we know just about the same thing that you know. The Embassy Room is pretty well barren now of supporters of Kennedy. The majority of the people here are the press. We have been told that that's it, we should move on. And actually that's about the story, tragic as it is, from here the Embassy Room at The Ambassador Hotel. Back to you Bob.

Ray Williams there. Boyd, as happened in the aftermath of the assassination of President Kennedy, the scene of shock and turmoil here was nationally advertised and televised, just as it was when Jack Ruby shot Lee Harvey Oswald. The television reporter said the man who fired the shots was just about ten feet from Senator Kennedy at the time. Reporters said that Stephen Smith, Kennedy's brother and campaign manager, also was shot. The American Broadcasting Company said its unit manager, William Weisel, was shot. Kennedy, of course, has been taken to a Los Angeles hospital and John D.

O'Connell, KNX radio newsman, is on that scene and will report to us just as soon as possible.

Of course, the major emphasis is on the results of the treatment of Senator Kennedy, but I would also like to know what happened to the other people involved—Steve Smith and this woman Ray McMackin said he saw shot in the head. They set up an emergency operating room apparently in one of the kitchens there at the Ambassador Hotel. Perhaps Ray Williams or Ray McMackin can get in there and see if we have any report on the others involved.

We understand that five doctors treated the senator before he was removed to the hospital. Another witness of the shooting said he fell down right away. He just lay there. Gabor Kadar, who said he was waiting at the rear exit to the room to shake hands with the senator, heard four or five shots and saw Kennedy and a woman fall to the floor. Kadar said Senator Kennedy was holding the right side of his chest and there was also blood on his head. A priest, before the senator was removed from the hotel...

Back to Kennedy headquarters for more information from Ray Williams.

Well, Bob, we have a young lady here that just informed us that Steve Smith, the Kennedy campaign manager, was not shot. If you would come over here, please, with us and let us have your information.

Uh, Stephen Smith, the senator's brother-in-law was not shot. I was right there at the time and he was standing up on a table. He was rather angry and rather distraught, but he certainly was not shot. He's perfectly all right. He seemed to be going with the senator to the hospital.

Fine. Thank you very much. And so, that clears up the point on Stephen Smith, Bob.

Thank you, Ray. We'll be standing by for any late information that you might have. A priest, as I started to say, before the senator was removed from the hotel, said he attempted to give the senator final rites of the Roman Catholic Church, but the surging crowd pushed him away. The priest said, I did give him the rosary and he clenched it tightly. As I was pushed away, there was blood on his head. The arrested man was hurried through a lobby, throngs still yelling and screaming at the news of the shooting. Kill him, lynch him, many in the crowd shouted, and many tried to reach the man, as we know from Bob Harris's report, there were some fights that broke out at that time. Police did manage to hustle him out of the lobby and down the stairs to an exit. We have no information as to who the man was. Two reports surfaced, one that he was Negro, another that he was Latin American. We will not know until police issue an official report on that.

I would imagine in this case, Bob, that the police are not going to be issuing very many reports for some time, in order to remove the carnival atmosphere that surrounded the assassination of President John F. Kennedy in Dallas. Police, as we say, captured a man believed to be the assailant, about twenty-five years of age, curly hair, and olive-skinned. They hustled him out through the lobby of the Ambassador Hotel, a shotgun at his back. The gunman was caught standing on some sort of a box. The shooting occurred in a small anteroom off the main ballroom. Only those near the door knew at first there had been a shooting. Five doctors, as we mentioned earlier, treated the senator before removal to the hospital. Several Kennedy supporters called for towels immediately after the shooting. A news reporter hastily stripped off a velvet tablecloth and rushed into the kitchen area, jammed with the shouting political supporters of the senator. The scene was complete confusion. Television cameramen and men carrying tape recorders stood on serving tables and tried to hold their equipment close to where first aid was being applied to the wounded, who were shot and bleeding. A tablecloth was used to stem the flow of blood from a blond man, who was stretched over a chair, his shirt up, bleeding profusely around the body. Kennedy's eyes were reported to be open. KNX news reporter Ray McMackin, who was an eyewitness to that seen said they were open, very definitely, but that he was not moving. The wife of one of the doctors said his condition seemed not to be critical, however. As we say, there have been a number of conflicting reports as to who was shot and who was not shot in this case. We hope to have information on it.

Bob, those reports that we have from the wire services seem to confirm what Ray McMackin said about a blond man being shot somewhere in the waist area. He told us that someone—one of the victims—may have been shot in the waist. He also told us about a young man being shot apparently in the hip. We also had the report of a seventeen-year-old youth being taken to Central Receiving Hospital by a friend, but apparently not seriously wounded. And the seventeen-year-old shot being in the hip would apparently clear up some of the confusion over some of the earlier reports that Senator Kennedy had been shot in the hip. We are waiting for John D. O'Connell to report from the hospital to try to give us some further information on Senator Kennedy's condition. There's absolutely no report available as yet on his condition.

This is the CBS radio network.

This is KNX, 1070 news radio, Los Angeles.

And this is Boyd Harvey, along with the entire election coverage here. Bob Arthur is with me in the studio as we're trying to piece together the facts that have occurred. A tragedy of major proportions at the

Kennedy headquarters here in Los Angeles, where Senator Robert F. Kennedy and apparently three others were shot by an unknown assailant, who has been apprehended by Los Angeles police. The condition of Senator Kennedy is still not known. He is at Central Receiving Hospital in Los Angeles. Bob?

Senator Kennedy's wife, Ethel, was at his side during that victory talk that he had made just prior to the shooting. He mentioned his dog Freckles and said the pet had been maligned during the campaign. Kennedy then waved to his supporters and was ushered backstage through a kitchen passageway en route to a room where he was to hold a news conference. And at that time, as best as we can piece together, four or five pistol shots rang out. Reporters ran into the kitchen passageway and saw the tumultuous scene and such exclamations as—oh my God, not again, no, no—cries from the crowd were heard. Stand back, give them room—others shouted as they tried to make space around the fallen candidate. KNX and CBS reporters are on the scene trying to glean what information they can, trying to get information from the Los Angeles Police Department, without success. We have been told that one of the other victims in this tragic episode at the Ambassador Hotel was an assistant director for the American Broadcasting Company. He was identified by ABC as Bill Weisel. His wounds were said to be superficial. He is from the Los Angeles area. This, the climax of a California presidential primary, regarded to be one of the most important and the important…

III.

There's been no new word on Senator Robert Kennedy's condition, no official word for more than eight hours now although a bulletin is expected shortly. There have been a lot of rumors. Now we will cut to the…to the hospital auditorium where apparently a bulletin is forthcoming.

Here is that bulletin.

I have a short announcement to read, which I will read, uh, at this time. Senator Robert Francis Kennedy died at one forty-four a.m. today, June sixth, 1968. With Senator Kennedy at the time of his death were his wife Ethel, his sisters Mrs. Stephen Smith, Mrs. Patricia Lawford, his brother-in-law, Mr. Stephen Smith, and his sister-in-law Mrs. John F. Kennedy. He was, uh, forty-two years old. Thank you.

And that was the word, Frank Mankiewicz making a very quick, a very short announcement that at one forty this morning Robert Francis Kennedy died at Good Samaritan Hospital in Los Angeles. He was forty-two years old. At his bedside, Ethel Kennedy and Mrs. Jacqueline Kennedy. Again, that very brief, very short bulletin. John… er, Robert Francis Kennedy died this morning at one forty at Good Samaritan Hospital in Los Angeles. In the press room at this time, reporters have rushed to the phones to make calls overseas to inform the rest of the nation what has happened here tonight. It was reported earlier that Senator Kennedy was very near death, apparently he was paralyzed on one side. And an earlier medical bulletin had said that there wasn't much hope for Senator Kennedy. He was not improving and conditions did not look good. So, very early this morning, his press secretary Frank Mankiewicz, his eyes…tears in his eyes, announced that

Robert Francis Kennedy, senator from Massachusetts, had died this morning at Good Samaritan Hospital at the age of forty-two. There's no word other than that. There is not much to say other than that except that America has lost a man, has lost a senator, and has lost an image that perhaps will not be replaced.

John Lennon

I.

John Smith is on the line and I don't care what's
on the line, Howard Cosell, you have got to say that we
know in the booth.

Yes we have to say it. Remember this is just a football
game no matter who wins or loses. An unspeakable
tragedy confirmed to us by ABC News in New York City.
John Lennon, outside of his apartment building on the
West Side of New York City, the most famous perhaps
of all of the Beatles, shot twice in the back, rushed to
Roosevelt Hospital, dead on arrival. Hard to go back to
the game after that newsflash. Frank Gifford?

Indeed it is.

...for scenes on December tenth, 1938, the first
scenes from the film Gone With the Wind. The burning
of Atlanta sequence lights the sky for miles...

We interrupt this program to bring you a special
bulletin from NBC News. Former Beatle John Lennon
is dead. Lennon died in a hospital shortly after being
shot outside his New York apartment tonight. A suspect

is in custody but has not been identified. Again, John Lennon is dead tonight of gunshot wounds at the age of forty. We now return to The Tonight Show.

In the latest report that we've got from the Associated Press, a police spokesman says a suspect in the killing of Lennon is in custody but he would give no further details. The spokesman did say it was not a robbery and that Lennon was killed most likely by a deranged person. It's eleven fifteen right now and we're gonna be doing a full hour of the Beatles in lieu of Boston on Moon Rocks tonight.

It's eighteen minutes after eleven o'clock on this, a rather gloomy Monday now for, uh, I was going to say for fans of music, but certainly anyone. John Lennon, former Beatle, shot to death in New York City this evening. It happened outside his apartment building on the city's Upper West Side. Lennon, who just had his fortieth birthday in October, was rushed by police to Roosevelt Hospital and pronounced dead upon arrival. According to police, the shooting took place outside the Dakota, the century-old luxury apartment building where Lennon and wife Yoko Ono lived. Police have a suspect in custody. They describe him as a, quote, local screwball. And they say there doesn't seem to have been any motive for the shooting. It was just two months ago that John released his first single in more than five years, ironically titled Just Like Starting Over. John Lennon, dead tonight in New York at the age of forty.

...I would imagine Beatle fans, at this point, just fans of John Lennon who, for no other reason, are all shocked and just felt they wanted to come here and... and be close to him.

...every other song for the remainder of this hour will be, uh, a track of music by the Beatles, as we kind of, uh, shall we say, think or exist in memorial for the death of John Lennon.

...his wife Yoko Ono was with him when he died. They do have a suspect in custody but the police have released no other details at this time. We will keep you posted on that situation of course.

John Lennon was shot tonight in New York and, uh, he is dead. And I think if you're looking for a radio station tonight that's not playing Beatles music, you will have a long hunt.

Stereo 101 doing a complete hour of Beatles songs, some written by Lennon some written by Lennon and McCartney, but John Lennon was a part of them all. It's eleven forty-nine right now and in case you haven't had your radio on, former Beatle John Lennon was shot and killed in front of his home on Manhattan's Upper West Side tonight. He was forty. Police said Lennon was shot three times about eleven o'clock tonight New York time and died in the emergency room at Roosevelt Hospital. His wife Yoko was with him when he died. A police spokesman says a suspect is in custody, but he had no other details available on the circumstances of the shooting. The spokesman did say that it was not a robbery and the person who shot Lennon was most likely deranged. A witness says a man in his mid-thirties with quote almost a smirk on his face gunned down the singer as Lennon, his wife, and several other people walked into the vestibule of the apartment building where the Lennons lived. The witness says the residents of the hotel told him the man had been in the vestibule for hours before the shooting. According to the witness, the man quote just walked out and shot Lennon. Lennon, who celebrated his fortieth birthday on October ninth, just released an album, Double

Fantasy, that he made with his wife in what was to be a comeback for the pair. Once again former Beatle John Lennon was shot and killed tonight at his Manhattan Upper West Side apartment. He was forty.

WWDC remembers a rock 'n' roll legend, John Lennon.

Standing in the dock at Southampton, tryin' to get to Holland or France.

...John Lennon was brought to the emergency room of the Roosevelt St. Luke's Hospital this evening shortly before eleven p.m. He was dead on arrival.

That is Stephan Lynn, a doctor at Roosevelt Hospital who just a little while ago confirmed that John Lennon has been shot and killed in New York City. Lennon and his wife Yoko Ono were on their way back from the Record Plant, a recording studio in New York City. Their limousine pulled up to their apartment building, the Dakota on New York's Upper West Side, and as they were walking into the Dakota, Lennon was shot apparently seven times in the chest. Lennon was shot reportedly by a white male who has been taken into custody. His identity has not been released but local police have described him as a local screwball and that's about all they've said so far. After Lennon was shot, he was taken by police car to Roosevelt Hospital in New York City. According to witnesses, there was blood all over the place but there was absolutely nothing that anybody could do. Lennon was pronounced dead on arrival at around eleven thirty p.m. Eastern Standard Time. With me is Source correspondent CD Jako, who has just come back from Roosevelt Hospital. CD, you had an opportunity to hear the doctors explain what happened. What did they say?

The doctor, Stephan Lynn, told us that there was

absolutely no chance for John Lennon. He said, in his medical opinion, that he was probably dead before he hit the ground. He had seven massive wounds in his chest at close range. The caliber of bullets he couldn't ascertain, but that the shots apparently ruptured most of the internal blood vessels and major organs. A policeman who was there, however, told me that Lennon was conscious after being shot. When he asked him—are you John Lennon?—Lennon replied, yes, before being put into the police car and rushed to Roosevelt Hospital. The doctor said he informed Yoko Ono, who was at the hospital at the time and that she, in his words, found the news very, very difficult to take. She has been rushed from Roosevelt Hospital, possibly back to the Dakota. He said it was massive chest wounds and that there was absolutely nothing anyone could do. We spoke to Jack Douglas, who was Lennon's producer on the new album Double Fantasy. He said that Lennon had been, as you said, at the Record Plant working on a new single and that that new single was to have been mastered by John Lennon tomorrow. Mr. Douglas obviously was completely distraught, as were most of the people there.

Thanks, CD. John Lennon, of course, was one of the architects of the Beatles, one of the most important rock 'n' roll bands in the history of rock 'n' roll—that probably goes without saying. Lennon had been in retirement for about the last six years, and in just the last few months, Lennon had gone back into the recording studio to record a new record with Yoko Ono called Double Fantasy. And again, John Lennon was shot dead tonight on his way inside his apartment in New York City.

We'll be doing a Devo/Hall and Oates concert

starting at twelve o'clock and any news about the Lennon situation that we have, we'll be interrupting the concert as soon as we get the news. Okay? Let's try some material from the former Beatle, John Lennon at KQ92.

...straight quote off the police report: a local screwball. And they say that there doesn't seem to have been any motive at all for the shooting. It was just a couple of months ago that Lennon released his first single in more than five years from the Double Fantasy album which he recorded with Yoko Ono. That record is now in the Top Ten. And in light of Lennon's death tonight, the title is ironic: Just Like Starting Over. Record producer Jack Douglas tells us that he and the Lennons had been in a studio called the Record Plant in midtown Monday night and that Lennon had left about ten thirty to get a bite to eat and then go home. A man named Sean Strub says he was walking south near Seventy-Second Street on the Upper West Side, when he heard four shots ring out. He said he went around the corner to Central Park West just in time to see John Lennon being put into the back of a police car. Strub said some people heard six shots. Others said Lennon was hit twice. The NYPD said he was hit in the back. Reports from the various wire sources say then he was taken to Roosevelt Hospital in Manhattan and pronounced dead on arrival. But they did try various resuscitation efforts and revival efforts for approximately fifteen minutes—even to the point of blood transfusions and special hookups to see if they could revive his heartbeat—but obviously to no avail. Other witnesses say that the assailant had been crouching in the archway of The Dakota, the Lennon's apartment complex in Manhattan. Police described the suspect—who is in custody at this point—as a pudgy

kind of man, aged thirty-five to forty with brown hair.
He was put into a police car with a smirk on his face—
that's a partial quote from the police report.

...CBS News. Former Beatle John Lennon was
shot and killed tonight in New York City. Police say a
man with the gun apparently had been waiting in the
entrance of the Dakota, the apartment building where
Lennon lived. Just as Lennon got out of the car, the man
opened fire. Lennon was brought to Roosevelt Hospital's
emergency room shortly before eleven p.m., according
to Dr. Stephan Lynn, director of emergency room
services. He was dead on arrival. Extensive resuscitative
efforts were made, but in spite of transfusions and many
procedures, he could not be resuscitated.

Where was he shot, Doc, and how many times?

He had multiple gunshot wounds in his chest, in his
left arm, and in his back.

Lynn said there were seven wounds in Lennon's
body, although he could not say how many shots were
actually fired. Lennon died, said Lynn, from damage to
the large blood vessels in his chest. He probably died,
Lynne said, almost instantly. Lennon's wife, Yoko Ono,
was with the singer when he was shot and later at the
hospital. According to Lennon's record producer, Jack
Douglas, Lennon had been at a recording session, then
had taken a break to go home to get something to eat.
He was shot in the entrance to his apartment. One
witness, Sean Strub, says the man who shot Lennon had
what was described as almost a smirk as he pulled the
trigger and he describes the suspect.

Between thirty and forty years old. He was kind of
fat. He didn't look like a groupie or, you know, anything
like that. He almost had a sort of smear on his face,
I mean, he was almost proud of what he had done

apparently. Uh, he scuffled with them...getting into the police car, uh, you know, his...his head was...was...was held high. He had...he had...kind of a sort of a smile almost. One person that lives across the street said he had seen the guy there on the sidewalk, like, all week, just been kind of hanging around. I think he intended to kill John Lennon. I mean I...I...I don't think it was a robbery or anything like that.

One police spokesman says the gunman, in his words, is a local screwball. Lennon has a single record in the Top Ten now. It's called Just Like Starting Over, from an album he recorded with Yoko Ono entitled Double Fantasy. It's the first single that Lennon has released in more than five years. It's been out just two months. Repeating, former Beatle John Lennon was shot and killed tonight in New York City. He was forty. More CBS News in a minute.

Initial police reports say the world renowned singer-songwriter was returning to his exclusive Manhattan apartment building, the Dakota, with his wife Yoko Ono when a man opened fire on Lennon. Eyewitnesses say that the man had been loitering in the area and started shooting the ex-Beatle for no apparent reason. Police say Lennon died shortly after the shooting. Police have a suspect in custody. Dozens of shocked fans, hearing the news on the radio, began arriving here at the hospital. Some spontaneously sank to their knees when Lennon's death was announced and began praying.

It's midnight. Good evening. I'm Michelle Diamond. John Lennon dead, shot down about ten p.m. tonight outside of his Manhattan apartment. And tonight on KCLD-FM, instead of Full Trackin' we have an hour of John Lennon and Beatles' music, in honor and memory of a great man, a great musician. Here's a track from the album Yesterday and Today, I'm Only Sleeping.

When I wake up early in the morning
Lift my head, I'm still yawning
When...

Good night.

II.

KQ92 at ten in front of seven. That is Jackson Browne from Hold Out. Well, I'm sure a lot of you people are kind of just getting the sleep bugs out of your eyes and are getting up to a new day. You might be interested to know that, uh, John Lennon was shot and killed yesterday as he was entering his New York apartment. We'll have a complete report from The Source in just a moment. And we'll have another special report from them that will occur at a little bit after seven thirty. And, of course, John Lennon is the morning feature. We'll be hearing from him next on KQ92.

Good morning. Former Beatle John Lennon was shot to death in New York City last night. It happened just outside of his apartment building on the city's Upper West Side. Lennon, who was just having his fortieth birthday, had been rushed by police to, uh, Roosevelt Hospital and there he was pronounced dead. According to police, the shooting took place outside of the Dakota—that's the century-old luxury apartment house where he and his wife Yoko Ono lived—and, uh, police have a suspect in custody. They described him as a local screwball. They say there doesn't seem to have been any motive for the shooting. When the suspect was put into the police car, he had a silly smirk on his face. It's a terrible tragedy. It's clear and thirteen degrees.

...they didn't want to make the move until four years later because, in his words, he quote, just didn't have the guts. After the Beatles broke up in 1970, Lennon continued writing songs and recording but in 1975, he dropped out for five years, saying he wanted to be with his son Sean and his wife Yoko Ono. It was not until last summer that he returned to music. His fourteen-song album Double Fantasy was released last month. Ironically the record—which is in the Top Ten—has a single which is titled Just Like Starting Over. This is from Abbey Road.

Something in...

...1971. Uh, good question for everybody to ask themselves, uh, when they are going over this event in their minds, I would say, particularly those of you that are hovering around thirty—between twenty-five and thirty-five maybe—ask yourself where you would be, what you would be thinking, how you would look, possibly, even today, if it wasn't for John Lennon?

...Mutual News. Former Beatle John Lennon was shot to death last night outside his apartment building in New York's Manhattan. Authorities say Lennon was rushed in a police car to a nearby hospital and was pronounced dead shortly after arriving. Doctors say he suffered seven severe wounds in his chest, back, and left arm. Mutual's Bernard Gershon has been following the story over the last few hours and says New York City police have now identified the suspect in the assassination of John Lennon as Mark David Chapman, a twenty-five-year-old man they believe is from Hawaii. New York City police believe the suspect came to New York a week ago and got an autograph from John Lennon on Monday afternoon. On Monday evening he shot John Lennon to death, they believe. This is John Hanrahan, Mutual News.

The music world was rocked by the sound of gunshots. John Lennon is dead. I'm Bob Madigan from The Source. John Lennon preached peace and nonviolence but last night outside his New York City luxury apartment building, John Lennon was gunned down by someone he probably thought was a fan. John and Yoko were taking a break from a recording session. They decided to head home for a late night snack. John walked from the limo to the apartment building and just as he was getting to the door, a man called out—Mr. Lennon! John turned. The man crouched into a combat position and unloaded his revolver. Five shots. He fell to the ground, mortally wounded, moaning, I've been shot. A short time later, John Lennon was pronounced dead at Roosevelt Hospital. In the moments before the police arrived, the doorman of the building kicked the weapon out of the way and the gunman just stood by. Police booked the man immediately on murder charges. Reporters stood by, waiting to find out more. In an emotionally wrought moment, the chief of detectives, James Sullivan, handled it with typical Jack Webb dryness.

We have arrested Mark David Chapman of fifty-five South Kukui—K-U-K-U-I—Street, Hawaii, for the homicide of John Lennon. He's a male Caucasian, tan complexion, five feet eleven, one hundred ninety five pounds, brown hair, blue eyes and he's twenty-five years of age.

Chapman reportedly had been hanging around the Lennon's home for almost a week, had even gotten Lennon's autograph earlier in the day. This morning, a crowd several hundred strong remains outside the Lennon's apartment. One of those—one of the few outside Lennon's tight circle of friends who made contact with Lennon—said, I delivered groceries to his apartment and he was a gentleman, he was a genius, he was an artist. He wasn't a politician that got shot. He was an artist and he was a great man. And, uh, God bless him, the Lord's with him. John Lennon is dead at forty. He was murdered last night outside his New York City apartment house. And that's news. I'm Bob Madigan from The Source.

And the weather for today, uh, chance of maybe a snow flurry this morning. It'll be mostly cloudy. Variable cloudiness and cold for tonight and tomorrow, twenty-three the high today, lows tonight down to about five. And tomorrow's high up to about twenty. Right now, we have fifteen degrees under a cloudy sky. Three minutes in front of seven o'clock. It's Wally Walker and, uh, well, we are gonna be playing more John Lennon tracks throughout the day today. As a matter of fact, I think I'm gonna do a John Lennon mini-concert right now. We have John Lennon as the morning feature, so you'll be hearing a lot of Beatles tracks and John Lennon's solo stuff throughout the morning. And we also hope to have that Source report for you at about seven forty, a little bit later on. And we're gonna start off with a twenty-five-minute jam from the man himself...

...and the world will live as one.

None of us will probably ever forget where we were and what we were doing when we first got word, when we heard the first reports that John Lennon, the man who gave birth to the Beatles was dead, felled by a lone gunman in front of his New York City home. Correspondent CD Jako has been with this story since it began and tells us of John Lennon's last day.

John Lennon and Yoko Ono left their apartment in New York's famous Dakota apartment building Monday afternoon headed for the Record Plant, a local studio. They were preparing to cut a new single. They may not have noticed a young man standing on the street. Neighbors say he had been hanging around the Dakota for several days. Only hours before, he had asked John for an autograph on an album. Lennon signed it. About ten thirty at night, John and Yoko returned from the studio. They stepped out of their limousine and started inside. The young man who had been hanging around, called to them. John turned. The young man was in a military firing position, both hands around the grip of a Charter Arms thirty-eight caliber revolver, his knees bent. He emptied the gun into Lennon. Lennon staggered several feet and collapsed in an office area.

I saw John and Yoko get out of the...get out of the limousine. They...they walked into the gate and, oh God... Let me just... And then I heard four or five shots. It was ear-shattering, ear-shattering. And then I heard Yoko...I heard a woman screaming...it was Yoko. She was screaming, help me!

Police cars raced to the Dakota, where officers found Lennon and lifted him into the back seat.

I saw the cops wrestling with the guy in the tan jacket and tinted, uh, tinted glasses. He had a kind of brownish-blonde haircut, heavyset, and they, uh, threw the cuffs on him and put him into a police car. Moments after that, I saw four officers carrying, uh, John Lennon and, uh, he was bleeding in the mouth and he looked very unconscious. And they put him into the back of the police car and they took him to the hospital.

The squad car was driven at top speed to the emergency room of Roosevelt Hospital, about a mile away.

Dr. Stephan Lynn is in charge of that emergency room.

John Lennon was brought to the emergency room of the Roosevelt St. Luke's Hospital this evening shortly before eleven p.m. He was dead on arrival.

Dr. Lynn broke the news to Yoko.

I did, uh, tell his wife that he was dead, and she was most distraught at the time and found it quite hard to accept.

Outside the Dakota hundreds of people, shocked and stunned, gathered in the warm New York night.

Woo! Woo!

All we are saying is give peace a chance...

Local New York radio stations played nothing but Beatles songs. The faithful lit candles, wept in each other's arms, laid flowers on the building grillwork, and cried for John Lennon and for that part of our youth that had died.

I imagine I started to cry and then I called my sister and she started to cry and it was horrible.

To a lot of people...something like this...you know...to millions of people, this has the impact of a presidential assassination. There's no question about it.

The first thing that went through my mind...like... this is for me like John Kennedy. Because I remember I was, like, seven at the time and I remember my parents crying and stuff like that. And this is the first time this kind of impact has occurred on me. I just...I don't know...I can't imagine the world without him. I really can't.

And amid the sorrow, confusion. Who shot John Lennon? Why? The young man who had been hanging around for a week just stood there after firing, threw the gun down and was grabbed by the doorman. He was taken to Twentieth Precinct headquarters nearby.

We have arrested Mark David Chapman of 55 South Kukui—K-U-K-U-I—Street, Hawaii, for the homicide of John Lennon. He's a male Caucasian, tan complexion, five feet eleven, one hundred ninety-five pounds, brown hair, blue eyes and he's twenty-five years of age.

Mark David Chapman, three names straight off the police blotter. Three names like many accused assassins—Lee Harvey Oswald. James Earl Ray. Mark David Chapman. Chapman flew to New York from Honolulu last week, allegedly with a thirty-eight caliber revolver police say he'd bought in Hawaii. He supposedly stayed at YMCAs and at local hotels and walked back and forth in front of the Dakota. Mark David Chapman has been charged with the first-degree murder of John Lennon.

I delivered groceries to his apartment and he was a gentleman, he was a genius, he was an artist. He wasn't a politician that got shot. He was an artist and he was a great man. And, uh, God bless him, the Lord's with him. John Lennon is dead at forty.

I read the news today, oh boy
About a lucky man who made the grade
And though the news was rather sad
Well I just had to laugh
I saw the photograph

John Lennon was born in Liverpool, October the ninth, 1940. By the time he was a teenager, his father was gone and his mother was dead. But in 1958, he struck up a friendship that was to change his life and all of rock music, because that's when he started playing with Paul McCartney, traveling in 1959 to Hamburg, Germany with a new band. John, Paul, drummer Pete Best, and guitarist Stuart Sutcliffe. Best was soon replaced with Ringo Starr and Sutcliffe died. Then back to Liverpool and a booking in a cellar club called the Cavern, where the band was discovered by Brian Epstein, the man who was to become the Beatles' manager. By 1963, the Beatles were performing for the Queen. A year later they were honored by being named members of the Order of the British Empire.

Oh yeah, I'll tell you something,
I think you'll understand,
Then I'll say that something,
I wanna hold your hand,
I wanna hold your hand,
I wanna hold your hand.

It was during this time that John first became a father. His son, John Julian Lennon, was born to his first wife Cynthia. But by 1968, that marriage was gone, Yoko Ono announcing to the world that she would bear Lennon's second child fully a month before his divorce was finalized. As Lennon's life was starting over, the Beatles were falling apart. In 1967, Brian Epstein died and along with him with the only thing keeping the band together. Writer Laurence Shames remembers those times.

Lennon in the sixties—although on the one hand, he was already tremendously wealthy and powerful and famous—was really in...in many ways, uh, terrifically naïve and an incurable idealist. And that idealism carried over into politics.

All we are saying is give peace a chance.
All we are saying is give peace a chance.
Ev'rybody's talking about Bagism, Shagism...

You know you have peace and staying in bed for peace. Do something that can't be smashed.

In the early seventies, John Lennon became the target of deportation. The U.S. government argued that he was ineligible for permanent residency in the country because of a 1968 drug conviction. Lennon fought the government and won.

This is the land of the free, right? And...and since the last hundred years, all the artists—major and otherwise—have been attracted to this country. And although initially it was on... I came as a Beatle, it was Yoko's influence that got me to look at it as a...a place to be in rather than just scoot in and run back with the loot.

Ultimately, it was only money that kept the Beatles together or at least kept the four members talking to each other. But in 1977, when they tried to end even that tenuous relationship, Paul McCartney remembers they couldn't even agree on that.

Basically, the three of us, uh, George, Ringo and myself, are ready to sort of get settled and ready to, uh, finish up and get it all cooled out, but, uh, John has got certain objections at the moment. And, uh, Lord knows what they are, you know, but, uh, he's been a bit funny at the moment.

Between 1975 and 1980, John Lennon didn't even record, turning his time and energy instead toward his personal wealth, buying homes, buying land, and even some prize-winning cows.

Whatever gets you through the night 'salright, 'salright
It's your money or your life 'salright, 'salright
Don't need a sword to cut through flowers oh no, oh no
Again, writer Laurence Shames.

When Lennon was singing in the streets and and... and giving his support to...to radical causes, he opened himself to a lot of criticism and...and he showed himself to have this sort of leftist working-class anger. Uh, in his later years, with his tremendous resources and...and his decision to invest and to try to build security for himself and his family, obviously that's something of a different side of him.

People say I'm crazy doing what I'm doing

Well they give me all kinds of warnings to save me from ruin

When I say that I'm o.k. well they look at me kind of strange

Surely you're not happy now you no longer play the game

People say I'm lazy dreaming my life away

Well they give me all kinds of advice designed to enlighten me

When I tell them that I'm doing fine watching shadows on the wall

Don't you miss the big time boy you're no longer on the ball

Soon John and Yoko came to call New York City their new home, buying into the very expensive and very exclusive Dakota Apartments.

One of the things, uh, that characterized him and Yoko was a real love-hate for the city and a love-hate for the whole idea of being that well-known and recognized. I think that although Lennon genuinely did want his privacy, he couldn't really just go somewhere where he would be obscure and unknown—he just…he just couldn't quite make that break.

Lennon really liked New York. He'd travel the streets in public, often showing up at local clubs, but always in the shadows, lurking more than strutting the way that some stars did. And now this star shines no more. The dream is over and with it, a part of us is also gone. One day before John Lennon died, he and Yoko recorded their annual Christmas message for the BBC.

And so this is Christmas and what have you done. Ha ha ha. Another year older etcetera, etcetera. It's nice to be here. Hi. We're pretty damn steady, as they say.

We're…we're in good condition. Thank you very much. It's great to talk to you and it's not kindness. We want to sell the record. And we want to tell the English to play Happy Christmas. Happy Christmas.

I read the news today oh boy
Four thousand holes in Blackburn, Lancashire
And though the holes were rather small
They had to count them all
Now they know how many holes it takes to fill the Albert Hall.

I'd love to turn you on.

Okay, you're on the air at CBS-FM. Do you have a question?

Uh, I have, uh, a few comments.

Okay.

I would like to say that I can't think of anyone who, uh, who deserves more to live for what they have given us. And, uh, another, uh, feeling that I have is that he is very, uh, consciously with us because he remains in my consciousness. I would also like to encourage the news media to never publish the name of the man who assassinated him.

Well, there's an idea because of the fact that that could be exactly what he's looking for. Unfortunately with the structure of news media that we have today, I would feel this would be pretty much impossible. Don't you Eric?

Yeah. I don't think there's chance in the world, although it's a nice thought.

Blackbird singing in the dead of night.
…the sound of a revolution.
…in so many ways. But now these days have gone…
…the English army had just won the war.

We'll be doing The Beatles from A to Z in a special

tribute. We'll be back with She Loves You in just a moment.

Okay and again, I'd like to say this is a bit of a tribute to John. He just had an interview in Playboy. I don't know if you've read it or not, but he mentioned a few things about death that I'd like to read to you. They asked him, what about death? What about rust never sleeps, Neil Young's thing about how it's better to burn out than to fade away? What did he say? I hate it, he said. It's better to fade away like an old soldier than to burn out. I don't appreciate worship of dead Sid Vicious or dead James Dean or dead John Wayne. It's the same thing, making Sid Vicious a hero. Jim Morrison is garbage to me. I worship the people who survived. Basically, he doesn't want to be worshiped. He wants to be remembered and I think that's about it. And of course everyone is taking this tragedy with shock and disbelief, but none probably harder than Yoko Ono, John's wife, who was said to be back at the Dakota Hotel in a state of shock. Of course, she was with John until the end. And also at the Dakota Hotel, it appears an impromptu memorial is being staged right now. There's hundreds of Beatles fans outside mourning. They'll probably be out, uh, all night, while still just a few feet away is the puddle of blood left from the attack. I guess it's kind of a reminder of the sickness of any violence, especially as senseless as this.

...I am, I'm only sleeping...

But it was always for peace.

Good afternoon, everybody. My name is Arne Fogel. John Lennon. The name itself is enough to bring about an instant flash of memories of a lifetime—not just his lifetime, I'm talkin' about your lifetime, too. Sitting as a kid in front of the TV screen during an early Ed

Sullivan show or an even earlier Jack Parr program, the memories of the radio stations as they would tease you by playing a choice cut or two from the latest Beatles album two or three days before it was available. And later on, when you first began to study him and his three partners, the revelation that they weren't newborn the first time you saw them with Sullivan, but that they had a history, long nights of playing for next to nothing in the dingy cellars of Liverpool and Hamburg, Germany.

... let me tell you about a girl I know. Woo. Thank you.

You learned that the voice of John Lennon was first recorded in 1961 and the first Lennon composition to be recorded was an instrumental also from 1961 called Cry For A Shadow.

Oh ain't she sweet...

Ain't She Sweet, Cry For A Shadow. It was all nearly twenty years ago. No need to go into a long rehash of the recent facts, suffice it to say that John Lennon at age forty is dead, cut down by an assassin's bullets in the flush of success of his first album in nearly six years. It's a tremendously sad time for those of us who treasured his work and career and for those like myself, who literally idolized the man and all he stood for. John was a brilliant man, a witty man, and perhaps the most important popular musician of the last thirty-five years. And in compiling the celebration of his life, I'm happy to report that I have been studying him, laughing a little, and listening a lot.

We didn't break up because we weren't friends. We just broke off out of sheer boredom.

Merry Christmas everybody.

Christmas cheer from John, Paul, George, and Ringo in 1963. A tribute to John Lennon today. We'll be here till four o'clock and we'll be doing another John

Lennon tribute tomorrow from two to four. Once again my name is Arne Fogel. His name is John Lennon.

And it tends to get into a format, you know? Because we were together much longer than the public knew us.

No reply.

And now a demonstration of the voice that over the last twenty years has often been described as one of the greatest rock 'n' roll voices in the history of the music: angular, lean, passionate, and infinitely emotive. Here's John Lennon interpreting the classic rock 'n' roll of composers other than himself.

Oh yes, wait just a minute mister postman
Wait, wait mister postman
Mister postman look and...

...He's in Bellevue Psychiatric Center in New York City right now. He won't be back to court until January sixth. That's because the judge says Chapman needs to go undergo psychiatric tests. Who is Mark David Chapman? He's twenty-five, five feet eleven, one hundred ninety pounds, brown hair, blue eyes. He'd been living in Hawaii for several years and before that had lived in Texas and Georgia. He worked as a security guard and a printer in Hawaii. He graduated from Columbia High School near Atlanta in 1973 and Lucy Badgett was a classmate.

I met him in eighth grade he was real, um, very straight, alright I mean, you know, he was very into, uh, school work and everything and, you know, just real straight. And then he just changed over the years. And I know he played in a band, a local band. Senior year he was more into religion and everything.

Just last week, Chapman supposedly borrowed two thousand dollars from a friend to fly to New York.

Robert Connell is the superintendent of Chapman's
Honolulu apartment building.

I didn't even know he was gone. In fact, uh, I just
saw him last week out in front...out in front of the
condominium and did not speak to him at the time, but
I saw him out there and I just couldn't believe that he
was in New York for this. So it was probably a...one of
those spur of the moment deals that he went to New
York for what purpose God only knows.

Mark David Chapman allegedly gunned down
Lennon with that snub-nosed revolver that he bought
October twenty-seventh in Honolulu. It was legally
registered at the police station down the street from
the gun shop. Richard Lester, who directed Lennon in A
Hard Day's Night.

It seems appalling to me that all this time nobody
has spoken about the problems of people having guns in
America and the problem that people can shoot a man
on the street and when... How many more public figures
will be killed before some sensible gun control will be
passed?

But the gun Chapman supposedly used was
registered. He was able to register it, Hawaii police say,
because he had no known narcotics record in Hawaii
and because he had no known felony record anywhere
in the country. So now Mark David Chapman is being
looked at by psychiatrists and John Lennon is dead.

The reaction to the word of Lennon's murder was
quick. With that story, Bob Madigan.

Almost as soon as the news of Lennon's death hit
the air, people began to flock to the Dakota. It was too
late to help—they knew that—but the vigil was sincere.
Signs went up almost immediately telling Yoko Ono
she was not alone in her grief. Flowers began to arrive

before dawn. Photos of John were tacked to the iron gates, gates closed to keep the milling mourners out of the luxury apartment building's courtyard. Through the night the crowd grew but remained quiet, talking among themselves in hushed tones. But every so often the emotions would become so intense that the crowd would break into song.

All we are saying is give peace a chance.
All we are saying is give peace a chance.
We don't love anyone as much as you.
When you're not near us, we're blue.
Oh John we love you.

Of the thousands gathered at the Dakota, everyone appeared bewildered. They couldn't believe the news. And many seemed to be looking for spiritual answers to what happened. That's why they were drawn to the fashionable address opposite Central Park.

I imagine I started to cry and then I called my sister and she started to cry and it was horrible.

To a lot of people something like this, you know, to millions of people this has the impact of a presidential assassination. There's no question about it.

The first thing that went through my mind...like this is for me like John Kennedy. Because I remember I was, like, seven at the time and I remember my parents crying and stuff like that. And this is the first time this kind of impact has occurred on me. I just...I don't know... I can't imagine the world without him. I really can't.

That feeling was shared by many others. Steve Soroka.

I guess I owe the man something. He's done a lot for me all these years and I don't know... I was in kindergarten when John Kennedy got shot and, uh, this day just keeps reminding me of the day Kennedy got shot. In fact, the impact is even twice as bad.

The main reason people gravitated to the Lennon's home was because they didn't know what else to do. They lost a friend, someone they had known intimately, though never met. Michael Allerman was one who stood in the rain.

All I have ever wanted to do was to meet him once. An autograph was secondary. But just to say thanks, because I thought I owed it to him and some guy just robbed me of my opportunity. It's just an awful, awful thing. And I...I mean I wish I could say something to Yoko. I mean, but no chance. I feel so bad for her.

Some of the people came from far away. Richard Perkins was at home in Ohio when he heard Lennon had been shot. He headed to the Toledo airport, flew to New York City, and took a cab to the Dakota to be part of the vigil.

I'm thirty-one years old and, you know, I've grown up with the Beatles since I was, like, in eighth grade, freshman year of high school, all through college, and, uh, you know, their life is part of mine. And, so, I had the opportunity, I figured I ought to come.

What were you doing when you heard?

I guess I just turned on the TV, uh, getting dressed and all of a sudden I heard about it and I was pretty shocked, uh, it's like a little bit of your life has been taken away from you.

Andrew Gelpman felt the same.

I just sat there for, like, an hour, just listening to the Beatles music and it's just, like, I didn't understand why anyone would want to do something, you know, just go out and kill someone because they're famous or something.

And the neighbors were shocked. Joe Plava lives but a stone's throw from the Lennon's apartment.

Well, for five years I've seen John and Yoko around a lot of times, very, uh, very nice people, always nod, always wave, always say something, just...just...just blows me away.

John Lennon was always a man of peace and love. Perhaps even for the man who took his life. In 1969, John was asked what he thought of capital punishment.

I can understand people thinking, uh, it's the only way to deal with them because I... I understand those people. I don't think they're right because it doesn't help murderers to hang them or help violent people to be violent to them. That's...it is all they understand really. It doesn't...I don't believe... Violence begets violence, you know.

Hours after his death, John's widow and son released a statement to the press and his many fans. Yoko and Sean said that there'd be no funeral for John, just time set aside for a silent vigil to pray for his soul. John loved and prayed for the human race, they said. Please pray the same for him. John Lennon died December eighth, 1980, and with him died a little bit of each of us.

And in the end the love you take is equal to love you make.

III.

Good afternoon. This just in. Thousands of people, many bearing flowers and candles in their hands and tears in their eyes gathered today in New York's Central Park for a last farewell to slain Beatle John Lennon. Millions more around the world joined the observance. Some attended local memorial services like the one in New York, others simply paused for a few moments as hundreds of radio stations joined in a vigil of silence and quiet music. Lennon's widow, Yoko Ono, asked that the world pray for John's soul for ten minutes, which started at two p.m. Eastern Standard Time. That was one hour ago. Police originally estimated as many as a half million people would attend the gathering in Central Park, but freezing temperatures and biting winds apparently kept away all but the faithful. For ten minutes, not a whisper or a word was heard in the heart of New York, the adopted home of the man who helped shape the thinking, singing, and living of an entire generation.

Space Shuttle Challenger

This is a special report from Channel 4 News. Good morning. The space shuttle Challenger is just a few seconds away from blasting off from the Kennedy Space Center near Cape Canaveral, Florida. Challenger finally getting ready to leave KSC, its launch delayed a couple of times because of weather and mechanical problems.

T minus 15 seconds...

That's the voice of Launch Controller Hugh Harris of NASA.

10...9...8...7...6... We have main engines starting... 4...3...2...1 and liftoff...liftoff...

Solid booster rockets kicking in...

...and liftoff of the 25th space shuttle mission and it has cleared the tower.

Challenger going into its roll. That's planned. Watch it spiral away from pad 39B. The first launch at 39B since the old Apollo days and the Skylab missions. It's chilly here in Florida. Icicles formed on the pad overnight. NASA engineers were concerned that they might have broken off during the launch and have affected the fragile heat protection tiles which protect the shuttle on its way back in during reentry.

...will travel down to, uh, 65% shortly.

I don't know what the effect might be yet. The astronauts might take a look later on during the mission.

Engines at 65%. Three engines running normally. Three good fuel cells. Three good APUs.

APUs are the auxiliary power units.

...257 feet per second, altitude 4.3 nautical miles, downrange distance 3 nautical miles.

It's always amazing to hear how quickly the shuttle moves. It's already more than four miles downwind as we just heard.

Challenger throttling up. Three engines now at 104%.

Challenger go with throttle up.

This shuttle mission will launch...

My God! There's been an explosion!

...velocity 2900 feet per second, altitude nine nautical miles. Down range distance seven nautical miles.

This is not standard! This is not something that is planned of course! I can see a solid rocket booster has broken away from shuttle Challenger. I cannot see the shuttle itself! I don't know if it's able to continue on one rocket booster! If it's able to jettison that rocket booster, it will be able to return to the Kennedy Space Center. Perhaps the shuttle engines are not enough to power the shuttle back down and they'll have to shut down.

We're looking very carefully at the situation. Obviously a major malfunction.

I hope they were able to survive! I hope the astronauts... We have absolutely no sign at all of the shuttle itself. All we saw was that one explosion only about a minute into the flight and we saw the solid rocket booster. Now here's something coming down. I don't know what that is! I don't think that that's the shuttle. I believe that that's a piece of debris that's coming back earthbound. I don't know. It's too small for the shuttle itself. Pieces falling out of the sky in the Florida morning. It's about twenty till noon in here Florida. There are contingency plans for the shuttle when something does go wrong, when something goes terribly wrong.

We have a word from the Flight Dynamics Officer that the vehicle has exploded. The director confirms that. We are checking with the recovery forces to see what can be done at this point.

We hear from Launch Control the vehicle has exploded, that's the orbiter itself. The shuttle Challenger, has exploded. We must...

Emergency procedures are in effect.

...assume that the crew is not alive. This is unheralded in the history of the space program! Ladies and gentlemen, I...I have covered space shuttle launches since the very first launch since before the first launch itself going way back and nothing like this has ever happened. Of course, there was the Apollo fire on the ground at the Kennedy Space Center—the Apollo 1 fire that killed three astronauts during a test run back in the 60s—but the shuttle program itself, to this time, has been untouched by any human problem. But this is a major problem which developed just a few moments ago. We could see it happen. There seemed to be some kind of a, uh, of a, uh, of an explosion aboard the rocket and all of a sudden all communication with the spacecraft was lost. Obviously it is going nowhere at this point. It looks as if debris is falling out of the sky. It almost appeared as if one of the solid rocket boosters or one of the spacecraft main engines went awry and something happened.

The Flight Director confirms that that we are looking at checking with the recovery forces to see what can be done at this point.

Oh! A great tragedy here! Christa McAuliffe the first private citizen in space. And the rocket has apparently exploded in the first minutes of flight.

Emergency procedures are in effect.

We're trying to get some information by listening to Mission Control.

We will report more as we have information available. Again I repeat we have a report relayed through the Flight Dynamics Officer...

Oh! A terrible thing!

...that the vehicle has exploded. We are now looking at all the contingency operations and awaiting word from any recovery forces and the downrange field.

A terrible thing! Debris falling out of the sky—falling slowly, painfully, tragically slowly—toward the Atlantic Ocean, just a few miles offshore. This flight was to have been such a bright chapter in the history of the manned spaceflight program, but it turned—in a flash of an instant—into a terrible, terrible tragedy. Of course Mission Control is only giving very scanty information as they scramble to try to find out what happened and to determine exactly what the status is. But as you heard them say, apparently the shuttle Challenger exploded within the first minute or so of flight and the fate of the crew members is unknown but it does not look good at all. The smoke just, um...crazy patterns in the sky, contrails from bits of debris going...going down toward the ocean, still falling. People in the grandstands—fans who had come from many miles from all over the country to wish Christa McAuliffe well—are sitting stunned, some of them leaving and shaking their heads in disbelief. We can see them from where we sit. It's an awful sight.

This is Mission Control Houston. We have no additional word at this time.

A terrible sight and one that I certainly had hoped that I would never have to see. NASA is looking at its contingencies at this point, but really it looks absolutely awful. It looks like there is no hope for any of the people aboard that flight.

Reports from the Dynamics Flight Officer indicate that the capsule apparently exploded and impacted in the water at a point of approximately 28.64° north, 80.28° west.

The worst fears of all of us who have covered space for a long time were realized this morning at Cape Canaveral.

We are waiting for verification as to the location of recovery forces in the field to see what may be possible at this point.

It appeared as if the debris from the exploded Challenger shuttle came down...

...and we will keep you advised as present information becomes available. This is Mission Control.

...just a few miles offshore. So of course they will be rushing to that area to try to see what they can find. A most terrible sight! The most terrible event! Naturally, a great deal of confusion as we try to piece together exactly what did happen and so far, there has been no specific word on what caused the malfunction—what caused the explosion aboard Challenger. It just seemed to be going perfectly as we watched it leave. We had thought all was going well, but within ten seconds after the launch of Challenger, a bright orange flash in the sky, one piece of the rocket seemed to break off from the rest of the main assembly. The main engines were still going on the Challenger itself and then this spark, it seemed, an ember almost flipped out to the side, and all of a sudden the smoke contrails were no longer straight and true. They were haywire and going crazy in the sky, and it was obviously and immediately apparent that an awful disaster had just been made. Still now we can see smoke as the wind starts to carry it—its patterns are dispersed in the bright blue Florida sky. It was an absolutely perfect day for a launch and everything seemed to be going well. And all of a sudden it happened. Christa McAuliffe and her crewmates, the pilot Mike Scobee; astronauts Michael Smith and Judy Resnik; mission specialist Ellison Onizuka—a mission specialist who'd flown before; Ronald McNair, a black American astronaut—a mission specialist who had also flown before; Gregory Jarvis, payload specialist; and, yes, Christa McAuliffe, the 37-year-old Concord, New Hampshire school teacher from Concord High, listed as a teacher observer on this flight, but of course she was more than that. She had been picked from over 10,000 teachers who had applied to be the first private American citizen in space—a mission which had been called for by President Reagan some time ago—and had spent many months in training for this moment. She and the rest of the crew had suffered many delays as the Challenger sat on the launch pad and waited out the weather for three days in a row, some mechanical snafus, which, uh, at the time we thought were embarrassing but now, of course, all of that has shrunk into insignificance alongside of this awful, awful tragedy. We can see people running from the, uh, the NASA headquarters building here...

This is Mission Control Houston...

...trying to get a better look at the water.

...recovery forces are in the field...

That news that the, uh...

...equipment, recovery vehicles intended for the recovery of the SRB in the general area. Those parachutes believed to be paramedics going into that area.

...paramedics are now parachuting into the Atlantic in the area where the debris from Challenger fell.

Chris, this is Judy Muller in New York.

To repeat, we had an...

We are following this with you.

...apparently normal assent with the data coming to all positions being normal up through approximately the time that the main engine throttled back up to 104%...

Mission Control saying now that everything on the instruments reading in the log centers seem to be looking all right.

...on the flight, there was an apparent explosion. The Flight Dynamics Officer reported...the tracking reported that the vehicle had exploded on impact with the water in an area approximately located at 28.64° north, 80.28° west. Recovery forces are proceeding to the area.

Chris, we just saw the parachutes going into that area.

Yes, Judy. Those are—according to Mission Control— they are paramedics who are parachuting into the area where the debris fell in the Atlantic.

...flight controllers are reviewing their data here at this point.

What they will find there is not known.

...we will provide you with more information as it becomes available. This is Mission Control Houston.

So the gleanings from that Mission Control report was that everything was looking normal as far as the instruments were concerned and that this apparent explosion aboard Challenger just happened in a flash with no forewarning and no instrument indication that anything was amiss as the Shuttle headed out downrange over the Atlantic in the first minute of its flight.

Chris, as you know, the voice of NASA, the voice

of Mission Control, whatever voice we hear, is always calm. But...but today, of course, we hear a different note of terrible...

Well it's a...it's a steely tone, I think, one that is, you know, a forced calm, the way you get when you are faced with an intensely emotional and tragic situation and try very hard to cover it. I must admit I feel the same way.

Here in New York we see the pictures on the monitor that NASA sends up of Mission Control and the faces in that room just tell it all.

Certainly do. Grim. Everybody sitting still, very little movement.

This is the first such first failure in 56 such manned space missions.

Never before has there been one like it and I very much hope that there will never be another one again.

We have come to accept this nominal idea, we're so used to things—except for minor glitches that we've been hearing about in recent launches—we're so used to this going almost flawlessly, that we, I think, have taken it for granted almost.

That's true. The hard part of this is, I think, that they plan so carefully for emergency situations. They can turn around immediately after launch and come back and land at the Kennedy Space Center if anything goes wrong. They can have an abort across the Atlantic at any one of numerous landing sites in western Africa. They can abort once around the world and then come down again in California or even back here at the Cape if they have an emergency in the first orbit. They can abort to orbit if something goes wrong just before they get there. They can go up and get into a preliminary orbit and then see what they're gonna do—as a matter of fact, they've done that once—but to have this happen without any warning whatsoever, uh, without any chance...

With all those computer backups telling them when anything goes wrong, even a hatch problem, it's... it's amazing that something wouldn't have shown up. I wonder in all that debris if they'll ever know.

I don't know. I don't know how deep the water is at that point, but I imagine that it's probably still well within the limits of the continental shelf and it's probably not too deep for salvage operations. There has been, of course, no official word on the fate of the crew, but from our vantage point and from what we could see—and we could see it at all, albeit it was several miles away—it did not look like they had a chance. It doesn't appear that any of them could've survived.

This would be tragic if it involved anybody—a member of NASA, an astronaut—but it is especially tragic with the first civilian in space aboard. I imagine her family was watching or is at the Cape.

Indeed they were, husband and children. And many dignitaries from all over the country and literally hundreds of educators and school kids who had come here to watch a person that had become something of a hero to them fly away into history. Perhaps history was made here today, but it's not the pleasant variety, not the glorious variety at all. This was to have been, of course, NASA's most ambitious year. They had more than a dozen Shuttle flights planned, which would far and away top the number that they've ever been able to launch in a single year before. What's going to happen to those plans now? What this is going to mean to America's manned spaceflight program or to the space program in general, of course, remains to be seen. Right now there's no talk of that, only of determining what happened and getting the official word on the fate of the seven man crew.

Chris, this happened just about a minute after launch. Did it not up to that point—since I was not there—could you describe what did it look like right up to that point?

Oh, it looked perfect, I mean, it looked like every other space shuttle launch that I've ever seen—and I've seen about ten, I think. Everything was going very smoothly. Mission Control was sounding very, very confident. The shuttle was climbing up into a very clear blue, cloudless Florida sky and all of a sudden... flash! The one bright flame that we can usually spot as the spacecraft carries out over the Atlantic for dozens and dozens of miles, became two bright flames. It looked almost as if one of the solid rocket boosters had exploded and split off from the spacecraft, sending it off course in a crazy, spiraling pattern for a few seconds. Then debris started to fall out of the sky into the sea.

Of course they have search and recovery people standing by for all these missions but it's almost become assumed that they would never go into action. It...it must be terrible for them too.

Well, they've always been ready and certainly they had people parachuting into the crash site, into the water, within, I would say, two or three minutes after the event, so they were ready and they did perform as they were supposed to. But there seems little chance that they'll find anybody alive out there.

For those who may have just tuned in, could you go over who the crew members are again?

Yes, of course. Frank Scobee, the commander of this mission, Michael Smith, the pilot, Judy Resnik, a mission specialist, Ellison Onizuka, a mission specialist, Ronald McNair, a black astronaut and also a mission specialist, Gregory Jarvis, who is a payload specialist and, uh, uh,

Sharon Christa McAuliffe, the 37-year-old high school teacher from New Hampshire who was to have been America's first private citizen in space.

And for those of us who have covered the space program for several years, some of those names are firsts in themselves. Ronald McNair, the first black astronaut in space, Judith Resnik was the second woman, I believe, in space or the third, she's among the first certainly, um, Dick Scobee, a veteran of space flights.

Yes he is. Well, Mission audio has been silent for a few minutes now and there has been no word specifically on what happened. All about...all that Mission people have said is that there was an explosion aboard the shuttle Challenger and, of course, the crew members at that point are very securely strapped into their seats. They have no ejection seats or anything like that, any kind of life saving device like that, which you might expect to find in a fighter plane when something like that happens. It's, uh, it's just the end. There is nothing they can do about it. They don't wear parachutes. There wouldn't be any way for them to get out of the spacecraft if they had the chance to do that anyway. They're sealed in there until they land.

As we see in NASA's optics, the Atlantic is just a stretch of blue calm belying what has just happened here. I see no debris. I see nothing as we scan the horizon there.

No. I'm looking at, uh, the video picture too and I...I can't see anything like that either.

You mentioned the solid rocket booster seemed to explode and burst away.

Well, I was, you know, tracking it with my eye and it seemed that something popped out to the side. Another flaming rocket piece popped away to the side of the spacecraft and the main body of it carried on for a little while longer and then started gyrating and twisting in the sky and finally started plunging straight down.

There was, of course, a crowd of spectators in the stands...

Hundreds of them.

...hoping to celebrate Christa McAuliffe's triumph today.

Yes, it was, uh, pretty grim. I looked over that way as soon as I could tear my eyes away from that terrible tragedy in the sky and people were just...just leaving, you know, what else could they do? They were getting out of the grandstands and walking away. Some of them seemed to be shaking their heads in disbelief, but there didn't seem to be any hysteria, no running. It was just like they could not believe what their eyes had just recorded in their minds.

A terrible thing for you and everyone there and I think, uh, it will take some time for the shock of this to sink in.

Yes indeed. Let's just recap here. We haven't gotten much additional information from NASA recently and we'll just say that within one minute of what appeared to be a perfect launch, there was an explosion this morning aboard the space shuttle Challenger carrying teacher Christa McAuliffe and six crew members into orbit. The rockets seemed to spin wildly in space for a few seconds and then plunged into the Atlantic.

We have with us now NASA spokesman George Diller and perhaps we can get some more additional information from him. George can you add anything to the reports we received from Mission Control?

Uh, not a great deal. One of the problems at this point is that before we can send any emergency team in to see what state the orbiter is in—if it is, in fact, intact—is that there is debris that falls from that altitude that takes a considerable amount of time to impact the ocean. Normally that is 15 minutes after any mishap. There is the possibility that we have gotten some paramedics into that general area but most aircraft and ships will stay clear until the period of the debris ends because the debris falling out of the sky, obviously, endangers the planes and the ships that would be going in to do whatever rescue attempt can be done. So we don't know what the state of the orbiter is at this time and as soon as, by calculation, we know that the debris has cleared, then we can go in and check the impact area, because we will know from Flight Dynamics Officer that it's past the point of vehicular impact.

Now, this very painful question: Is it possible that anyone could have survived an accident like this?

It depends on whether or not the orbiter is damaged. If the orbiter did not explode and it is not seriously damaged, it will float for a period of time. That's why we try to get crews in as soon as we can because there is, I believe, about an hour, where there's no problem.

Gary, I guess President Reagan is watching—as we all are—in shock and disbelief, waiting to find out if there's any possibility that the orbiter might have landed intact. And, going back to Chris, that was the question I suppose we'll know, um, soon—will we not?

Well, it's difficult to say. If there is the possibility that the orbiter could have remained intact and have plunged into the sea intact, then it becomes a question of finding the orbiter: How deep is it? How quickly can we get divers down there to see what's going on? Now, don't forget, at the same time, even if the orbiter were to have, um, survived the explosion intact, it was falling from an enormous height. I don't know exactly how high it was at the at the moment of the explosion but, it was falling from a very, very great height and gaining speed as it came down and, uh, when it impacted on the water, it would be sort of like driving into a brick wall. It's not just, uh, a swan dive— it would be falling and impacting with enormous force on it. So, even if it did survive intact, what could be the likelihood that anyone could have survived the fall from that height? I don't know the answer to that and NASA, of course, is spending every possible ounce of energy to try to find the answer to that question. We can hope for the best but it does not look good.

How long do you think it will be before they know one way or the other?

Well, he said it was 20 miles offshore or so and they do have rescue teams on the site. I don't know how they are equipped or whether they're equipped to do any deep sea diving. It takes about 15 minutes for something to fall from the sky at that altitude. It appeared to my eye—as I watched the debris falling toward the Atlantic— that it was approaching the surface of the water much more rapidly than that, but of course I could be wrong. I did not see anything large enough to appear to be the main body of the shuttle. Now we do have here in our studios with us now Jim Rivers who is with WKXL in Concord, New Hampshire. Jim, can you give us your impressions of what's happened and how the folks in Concord must feel?

Well, as you can expect, Chris, utter, utter shock at the, uh, tragedy of the situation. At Concord High School, uh, party hats and noisemakers and New Year's Eve types of things had been handed out. The student body had lined into the auditorium and it had become just a festive affair. From the moment the countdown got down to the final minute, the cheering began and it began to build until liftoff. Even a minute in, when the explosion came, there was cheering...and then all of a sudden... silence. Just moments ago, at Concord High School, the auditorium was littered with party hats and noisemakers. The students have filed out. The media, too, has been asked to leave the high school. The situation right now, as you would expect, in the city of Concord, not only for Christa McAuliffe but for the entire crew is...is...just pray to God that they're somewhere...

And the state of New Hampshire and the nation and—without a doubt, the entire world—is mourning this great tragedy.

Jim, any further insight into the way that Concord feels about this?

Well, Chris, I've been in contact with the city and it's...it's desolate. We talked to a caller on a talk show this morning and he said you would've thought that the town had been evacuated. Everybody was in front of TVs. So this is an event that people aren't just going to read about in the papers. It's something that everybody saw as it happened. And a lot of us in Concord are rookies seeing this, so when we saw the ball of fire we thought it was part of the whole event. And everybody's just sitting back and praying and hoping that there are seven people out there in the water somewhere. We've had a couple of calls in the studio in the last few minutes from concerned people. We had a call from a young boy who wanted to talk to someone. He asked if the apple had anything to do with it.

A member of the closeout team outside the rocket just before Christa McAuliffe got aboard this morning handed her an apple for the teacher. This young listener said—did anyone check the apples? So everybody's saying, why? What happened? What went wrong?

Chris, anything new from the Cape at all?

No Judy. It's really...it's calm here. Of course, we're sitting in the position from which we watched the space launch and it's a benign looking scene. About the only reminder of this tragedy within our eye's range is still the traces of those awful clouds that formed as the rocket exploded, still drifting in the sky, with no wind today to push them out of the way.

Things have just been going so badly for NASA and this is bound to set back the program. It would seem to me to be a long time before they send another civilian into space.

I don't think they'll be sending anybody into space for quite a while, Judy.

The last tragedy anywhere near this magnitude, of course, was the Apollo launch explosion. That was on the pad in which Gus Grissom, Edward White, and Roger Chafee were killed.

Yes, that was not a space flight. It was a training mission. It was a static Apollo module and the situation at that point—I think it was in 1967, if I'm not mistaken—was that there was a flash fire inside the command module, the Apollo command module, and before anybody knew what was happening and they could get them out, they were all asphyxiated and subsequently burned to death.

It was, interestingly enough, January 27, 1967.

Nineteen years ago. Exactly. There never been to my, uh, recollection any space flight tragedy of this dimension in the history of manned space flight for any nation. Of course the United States has never had anyone die in flight before, only those, those three—Chafee, White, and Grissom—who died on the pad here at Cape Canaveral. But the Soviets did have a couple of losses of life. I seem to recall sometime back—and I'm picking my memory for 15-year-old details here—but two cosmonauts were killed on a landing attempt. Something went wrong there and, of course, the Soviets are very hesitant about explaining publicly any tragedies. And even at the time there was very little information on that, but I do recall that happened. And that's about the worst previous in-flight manned space incident I can think of.

The debris does appear to have cleared at this time and they are sending in crews now to see whether or not the orbiter may by some chance be intact. And we don't know what state the orbiter itself is in so it's premature to speculate that we've lost it. We really don't know.

Given a fall of a...of a body that massive from that great altitude, is it possible it could have survived the impact in one piece?

Well, it depends on, you know, what the nature of the explosion was. Was it the solid rocket boosters or was it the orbiter? The orbiter could float for up to an hour if it's intact and not damaged. If the orbiter is damaged, how long it will float for is undetermined. It is NASA's hope that somehow, some way, the orbiter survived the explosion intact and might have been able to perform a successful ditch into the Atlantic. Rescue teams are moving to the craft site now and what they will find there is anyone's guess at this point. But from the eyeball view of it and from all indications so far—the lack of communication and anything else—it did not appear that anyone survived, uh, the explosion this morning.

Well, it was nearly an hour ago that shuttle Challenger, less than a minute and a half off the launch pad exploded in flight. The fate of the crew is still officially unknown. It was an awful long way down and the water there is quite deep—they're about 20 miles offshore—so it's going to be a long time before we get any from information on what has happened to the crew, but it does not appear too bright for their survival at this point.

So far the main recovery efforts underway are by the Coast Guard. They have a couple of ships in the area there along with aircraft to see what they can achieve there. At the same time, the Navy says two ships that happened to be in the general vicinity—they weren't there on station, they weren't there on duty, but they were in the general location—are now rushing toward the disaster area. One, we're told, is about 45 minutes away—a hydrofoil—which carries about 21 men. Another ship, a U.S. guided missile frigate with 200 men is steaming toward the location, but that ship is a good two hours away. A Navy official said that, as best they could tell, there were no Soviet ships in the immediate area. We don't know if the Soviets at this time were off the Florida coast—well off the Florida coast I should say—watching this launch. They have been out there in the past. Whether they were there this time is unknown. And as best the Navy can tell, there were no ships anywhere around because area had been cleared prior to the launch.

Chris, any new news?

No, nothing new Judy, only to say that at this point, nothing is known for sure. It just happened. We did, however, receive word that the Senate has scheduled a prayer session for this afternoon. Of course it seems so long—so agonizingly long—since this happened that those of us were waiting and hoping wonder what's going to happen now. What will happen now?

It's hard to say. What was immediately apparent was what we could see with our eyes. This rocket appeared to be going so well without warning—to the eyes or to instruments of any kind—then it just blew apart in the air.

Christa McAuliffe was, of course, aboard that flight—

the first citizen in space, the first teacher in space—and she was thrilled when she accepted her choice as the first private citizen to fly on the shuttle. The parents of the New Hampshire teacher, of course, were on the scene at the Cape when the disaster occurred. They stared in utter disbelieve as they watched the shuttle explode. There was cheering before the explosion, there was happiness, and then—oh my God! Oh no, said one. And with looks of shock, the Corrigans—Edward and Grace Corrigan of Framingham, Massachusetts, the parents of Christa McAuliffe—were taken to another room by NASA officials. She had said long before the flight that what she really wanted to do—the real reason that she wanted to go into space—was to demystify NASA and space flight. She herself said it's a safe place to be.

I want to prove that this is as safe as walking across the street.

Christa wanted to show ordinary people and generations of young Americans that there was a place for them in space and a reason that they should be going there, and I think her words are ironic and, uh, especially tragic today given the scope of this disaster which we have seen before our eyes. This from her White House speech:

It's not often that a teacher is at a loss for words. I know my students wouldn't think so. I've made nine wonderful friends over the last two weeks. When the shuttle goes they might be one body, but there's going to be ten souls that I'm taking with me. Thank you.

Columbine

Jefferson County 911.

Yes. I am a teacher at Columbine High School. There is a student here with a gun. He has shot out a window. I believe one student, uh, um, um, I've been, um, I don't know if it's…I don't know what's in my shoulder, if it was just some glass he threw or what.

Has anyone been injured, ma'am?

Yes! Yes!

Okay.

And the school is in a panic and I'm in the library. I've got… Students down! Under the tables, kids! Heads down! Under the tables! Um, kids are screaming, the teachers, um, are, y'know, trying to take control of things. We need police here.

OK, we're getting them there.

Can you please hurry?

Who is the student, ma'am?

I do not know who the student is.

Okay.

I saw a student outside, I was in the hall—[sound of shots being fired out in the hall; Patti begins to panic] Oh, dear God! Okay! I was on hall duty, I saw a gun. I said, what's going on out there? And the kid that was following me said it was a film production, probably a joke, and I said well, I don't think that's a good idea and I went walking outside to see what was going on. He pointed the gun straight at us and shot and…my God! The window went out and the kid standing there with me, I think he got hit!

Okay.

There's something in my shoulder.

Okay. We've got help on the way, ma'am.

Oh, God! Stay on the line with me. Oh, God! Kids, just stay down!

Do we know where he's at?

I'm sorry?

Do we know where he's at?

I'm in the library. He's upstairs. He's right outside of here.

He's outside?

He's outside of this hall.

Outside of the hall or outside…

He's in the hall. I'm sorry. There are alarms and things going off. There's smoke. My God! Smoke is, like, coming into this room.

Okay.

I've got the kids under tables here. I don't know what's happening in the rest of the building. I don't know. I'm sure someone else is calling 911.

Yes, we have a lot of people on… Okay. I just want you to stay on the line with me, I…we need to know what's going on.

Okay.

Okay?

I am on the floor.

Okay. You've got the kids there? Okay?

In the library. And I've got every student in the

library… ON THE FLOOR! You guys STAY ON THE FLOOR!

Is there any way you can lock the doors?

Um, smoke is coming in from out there and I'm a little…[More shots, louder this time] The gun is right outside the library door, okay? I don't think I'm going to go out there. Okay?

Okay. You're at Columbine High School?

I've got…I've got three children…

Okay. We've got it.

Okay, um, I'm not going to go to the door. He just shot toward the door. I've got the kids on the floor, um, I got all the kids in the library on the… Yes. I mean… He's… I can't believe he's…not out of bullets! He just keeps shooting and shooting and shooting!

Okay. Yeah. We have a police officer on scene. Okay. Just try and keep the kids in the library calm. Is there any way you can block the door so no one can get in?

I think… I do not…

Okay.

I… Yeah. I guess I can try to go, but, I mean like, he's right outside that door. I'm afraid to go to the door.

That's okay.

That's where he is. I'm afraid to go there.

Okay.

Okay. I told the kids to get on the floor. I told them to get under the tables. All of the children are on the floor, under the tables. Um, um, yeah, they're all under the tables.

Okay. As long as we can just try and keep…

…I'm just trying to keep calm. No one's saying a word.

Okay. As long as we can keep everyone there as calm as we can…

I hear some yelling out there going on right now!

Yeah, we've got alarms going off now as well. Yeah, there's alarms. This room is filled with smoke!

Okay. Okay. Keep everyone low to the floor.

Yeah. Yeah. Everyone's... Uh, everyone stay on the floor! Stay on the floor! Stay under the tables! Um...I...I don't know. I...

Okay, I know. Just...

I don't know. I didn't... I said...what...what has that kid got? He was outside at the time. And...and...and, um, I was on hall duty. [Explosion] Oh, God! Um, he was going like woo-hoo-hoo! They're getting shots off.

Who was the student?

I do not know who the student was. I don't even... I saw him. He was wearing black. He looked very large, um, male student, um, he was out there shooting. [Another explosion] It looked like he was...out shooting and somebody... I said what is that? [Another explosion]

Mm-hmm.

I said what's going on out there? Well it's probably a cap gun. Probably a video production, you know, they do these videos...

Right.

And the kids... Well, I said, that's not, you know, a play gun, a real gun, I was goin' out there to say no, and I went... [Another shot, very loud] Oh, my God! That was really close! That just rattled me.

Okay.

One of the shooters: YEAH! [Another shot]

[whispering] Oh, God. I'm really...frightened. [More shots, extremely close] I think he's in the library.

What's your name, ma'am?

[whispering] My name is Patti.

Patti?

[whispering] He's yelling everybody get up right

now. [More shots] He's in the library. He's shooting at everybody.

Okay. I have him in the library shooting at students and…the lady in the library, I have on the phone… Okay. Try to keep as many people down as you can.

World Trade Center

I.

This just in. You are looking at obviously a very disturbing live shot there. That is the World Trade Center, and we have unconfirmed reports this morning that a plane has crashed into one of the towers of the World Trade Center.

We are right now just beginning to work on this story, obviously calling our sources and trying to figure out exactly what happened. But clearly, something relatively devastating happening this morning here on the south end of the island of Manhattan.

This is, once again, a picture of one of the towers of the World Trade Center.

And as we can see in these pictures, obviously something devastating that has happened. And again, there are unconfirmed reports that a plane has crashed into one of the towers there. We are efforting more information on the subject as it becomes available to you.

Right now we've got Sean Murtagh—he is our

producer—on the telephone. Sean, what can you tell us what about you know?

This is Sean Murtagh. I just was standing on the vice president of the vice president of finance.

Sean, we're on the air right now. What can you tell us about the situation?

Hello?

Yes, Sean, you are on the air right now. Go ahead. What can you tell us?

I just witnessed a plane that appeared to be cruising at slightly lower than normal altitude over New York City, and it appears to have crashed into—I don't know which tower it is—but it hit directly in the middle of one of the World Trade Center towers.

Sean, what kind of plane was it? Was it a small plane, a jet?

It was a jet. It looked like a two-engine jet, maybe a 737.

You are talking about a large passenger commercial jet.

A large passenger commercial jet.

Where were you when you saw this?

I am on the twenty-first floor of five Penn Plaza.

Did it appear that the plane was having any difficulty flying?

Yes, it did. It was teetering back and forth, wingtip to wingtip, and it looks like it crashed into, probably, twenty stories from the top of the World Trade Center, maybe the eightieth to eighty-fifth floor. There is smoke billowing out of the World Trade Center.

Sean, what happened next? Does it appear to you that the plane is still inside the World Trade Center?

From my angle—I'm viewing south towards the Statue of Liberty and the World Trade Center—it looks like it has been embedded in the building. I can't see, from my vantage point, whether it has come out the other side.

Sean, what about on the ground or any debris that has hit down there?

My vantage point is too far from the World Trade Center to make any determination of that.

Did you see any smoke, any flames coming out of engines of that plane?

No, I did not. The plane just was coming in low, and the wingtips tilted back and forth, and it flattened out. It looks like it hit at a slight angle into the World Trade Center. I can see flames coming out of the side of the building, and smoke continues to billow.

Generally, is that a trafficked area in New York for aircraft?

It is not a normal flight pattern. I'm a frequent traveler between Atlanta and New York for business, and it is not a normal flight pattern to come directly over Manhattan. Usually, they come up either over the Hudson River, heading north, and pass alongside, beyond Manhattan, or if they are taking off from LaGuardia, they usually take off over Shea Stadium and gain altitude around the island of Manhattan. It is rare you have a jet crossing directly over the island of Manhattan.

For our viewers who are just tuning in right now, you are looking at live pictures of the World Trade Center tower, where, according to eyewitness Sean Murtagh, the vice president of finance and eyewitness to what he describes as a twin-engine plane or possibly a 737 passenger jet, flying into the World Trade Center. It appears to be still embedded inside the building.

Sean, are you in a position to hear whether any

sirens are going, any ambulances, any response to this yet?

Not from my vantage point. I am probably one and a half to two miles miles from the World Trade Center.

It is a remarkable scene. Flames are still coming out of the windows, black smoke is billowing from what appears to be all sides. Obviously, windows are shattered and steel is jutting out from the structure right now.

Sean, we are looking at these pictures.

Yes. I see them in my office. I have them on all my TVs.

And you are telling us you believe the plane remains embedded?

I can't tell from my vantage point.

Sean, thank you so much for your eyewitness account there.

Right now, we want to go to our affiliate NY1, reporting on this as we speak.

…a little girl in his arms?

Did you see what happened, sir? Did you see what happened? What happened?

I was in the PATH train, and there was a huge explosion sound. Everyone came out. A large section of the building had blown out around the eightieth floor.

Was it hit by something, or was it something inside?

It was inside.

It was inside.

It looked like everything was coming out. All the windows and the papers.

What is on the sidewalk?

I didn't see anything. I just ran, and everyone on the passenger train just ran. I don't know if anyone was hurt, but I assume they were because the windows were all blown out.

Thank you.

You have to assume a very, very terrible situation if that is indeed the case, because I'm sure there were people up there.

We have lost… Again, our transmitter is on top of the World Trade Center. So we, apparently, have lost contact…

Again, you are looking at pictures now. We understand from our vice president, Sean Murtagh, who was an eyewitness to this, that a commercial jet has crashed into one of the towers of the World Trade Center. You can see the smoke billowing out. There are flames billowing out there, a commercial jet crashing into one of these towers. At this point, we do not have official injury updates to bring you. We are only now beginning to put together the pieces of this horrible incident.

We want to go to an eyewitness on the telephone right now.

Jeanne, what can you tell us what you saw?

I can tell you that I was watching TV, and there was this sonic boom, and the TV went out. And I thought maybe the Concorde was back in service, because I've heard about that sonic boom. And I went to the window—I live in Battery Park City, right next to the Twin Towers—and I looked up, and the side of the World Trade Center exploded. At that point, debris started falling. I couldn't believe what I was watching.

Can you hear anything from your position now— ambulances, sirens?

Absolutely. Positively. There are crowds of people downstairs in Battery Park City. Everybody's come out from the buildings. This is the financial area in

Manhattan. There are a lot of fire engines—I can see them from my window.

Jeanne, I don't know if you can tell which tower it is that is on fire, or the kinds of services that are inside that tower.

I can't tell what is inside. It's the northern tower versus the southern tower, and it seems to be all sides of the building, from what I can tell. The west side, the south side, and it looks like smoke's coming from the east side as well.

Jeanne, can you see any of the debris currently on the ground area?

Absolutely. It's continuing to flutter down like leaflets, and at first there was tons of debris, and it continues to fall out. And it looks like these uppermost floors are definitely on fire.

Can you see any actual people in that area who may have been…may have been hit by any of this debris or were not able to get out of way? Can you see any crowds that are maybe too close to where they should be? Anything like that?

No, I don't think so. It's not a highly trafficked area at the base of the World Trade Center. So that is one fortunate thing.

Jeanne, we are continuing to look at pictures of this devastating scene. Sean Murtagh, vice president of finance, witnessed what he described as a twin-engine plane, possibly a 737. He was almost absolutely sure it was a large passenger jet that went into that. Jeanne, you are saying you didn't see anything initially. You didn't see a plane approach the building?

I had no idea it was a plane. I just saw the entire top part of the World Trade Center explode. So I turned on the TV when I heard them say it was a plane. It was really strange.

Were you living in New York during the World Trade Center bombing?

No, I wasn't.

Fortunately so. When you say a sonic boom, did you feel anything? Were things shaking in your apartment?

Yes, you could feel it. It was a gigantic sonic boom. The TV went off for a second and went back on. And the windows—you felt the vibrations on the windows.

You were saying it's not a highly trafficked area usually. You can guesstimate how many people may be in an area like that at this hour of the morning?

It would be hard to say. There is a huge courtyard between the two World Trade Center buildings, and the only issue might have been tourists or business people out in this courtyard area, and they possibly would have been hit. But the people that are immediately around the base of the World Trade Center, I would say, at any given time, you're talking about maybe 20 or 30 people at best.

We were talking with Sean Murtagh earlier, and he said this is not normally an area where you would see some sort of aircraft, certainly, obviously, that low. That is not a high traffic area in terms of flights?

I don't know about flights. I have a balcony down here in Battery Park City, and they have that needle sticking out of the top of the World Trade Center, and I have always wondered if anyone would get too close to the building and accidentally bear into it.

Jeanne, tell us a little bit about that area and how emergency crews would be able to access that area? Would that be relatively difficult or easy to access for emergency people?

I would imagine it would be slightly difficult

because to get around the base of the World Trade Center building there is really only the one street entrance. The other sides of the building are surrounded by other buildings in the courtyard, and so it's just the West Side Highway, the one major street that runs up the west side of Manhattan that makes it accessible for the fire engines. And you know, it's amazing to sit here and watch this building on fire and you've got this tiny little fire engine that I'm watching.

That's all you see right now, is the one fire engine?

Well, where the fire engines are it's a little bit obscured by other buildings.

Right. Jeanne, let me ask—I know I'm asking you to be a bit of an expert on the World Trade Center—but there's a famous viewing deck for tourists on one of the towers. When you say that this is the North Tower, is this the one that services a lot of the tourists to get to the view and get to the restaurant at the top?

As a matter of fact it is. And, as I'm sure you can see, there's a ton of smoke coming out right now.

I'm just guessing, the fire seems to be worse on—it looks like it's about fifteen floors down from the top of the building.

Yes. One of the eyewitnesses—one of our affiliates I was talking to—said that she thought this was on the eightieth floor. We know there is an open-air deck one hundred ten stories high and the glass enclosed observatory is on the one hundred seventh floor. So there is the possibility that people may very well be trapped up there.

Now, when you say a huge hole, one of our earliest witnesses, Libby Clark, said not much of the plane came down off the building, much of it went...

No, it went totally into the building.

It's in the building, from what you can see?

Right, yes.

Now, can you see if there is a lot of debris downstairs, Jeanne?

No, because it looks like it's inverted. With the impact everything went inside the building.

Inside?

The only thing that came out was a little bit of the outside awning. But I'd say the huge…the hole is… Let me just get a better look right now…

OK, go ahead.

I'd say the hole takes about…it looks like six or seven floors were taken out.

And there's more explosions right now! Hold on! People are running. Hold on!

We should hold on just a moment. We've got an explosion inside.

The building's exploding right now! You've got people running up the street!

Hold on, I'll tell you what's going on.

OK, just put Jeanne on pause there for just a moment…

OK, the whole building exploded some more, the whole top part! The building's still intact, people are running up the street! Am I still connected?

This would support probably the idea that perhaps the fuselage is in the building. That would cause a second explosion like that.

Well, that's what just happened then.

That would…certainly…

People are running up!

We are getting word that perhaps…

OK, hold on, there are some people here… everybody's panicking!

All right, Jeanne, you know, let me put Jeanne on hold for just a moment.

OK. How much longer are we staying on? I'm inside of a diner right now.

Well, Jeanne, you know what, if you could give us a call back… I just… Don't panic here on the air.

Goodbye, Jeanne.

We thank you very much for your insight. Why don't we take a quick look at traffic. Debbie, I'm sure traffic has got to be a mess. Debbie, are you there?

Yes I am. Um, traffic is a nightmare. All the bridges and tunnels getting into the city are being shut down right now. Lincoln, Holland, George. Shut. Forget about it. Turn around. Go back home. Fifty-ninth Street Bridge. Closed. Brooklyn Bridge, Williamsburg, Brooklyn Battery Tunnel, again the Manhattan Bridge, uh, everything being closed heading into the city. And of course you want to avoid the area of the Twin Towers right now. You have tons of emergency vehicles there. And also all the area airports are closed, uh, Newark, Kennedy, LaGuardia, all the major airports are shut down. So again, avoid this area of the city. It is a nightmare.

Thanks, Debbie. Best to stay right where you are. And a reminder to folks trying to watch this on TV in the metropolitan area. Most of the television broadcast antennas are on top of the World Trade Center towers, so you're most likely not going to be able to get a picture. Your best bet is satellite dish or radio.

And we're showing you live pictures now. Smoke and fire taking place in both towers of the World Trade Center. It is a terrible scene. People are just walking down the street with their hands covering their mouth in disbelief. They can't believe it. And then you hear the sirens and people screaming as they look up at the building and see people trying to get out and some people jumping. Now, the EMS is here, fire personnel, police, everyone's here trying to keep calm and get everyone away from the building and keep it safe. Let's listen.

...but, um, I did see someone jump. I did. And I talked to someone and in her own voice you could hear it and she just lost it...

...they...they're throwing themselves off the building. Oh my God.

II.

There are explosions right now! Hold on, people are running! Hold on!

Hold on just a moment! We've got an explosion inside!

The building is exploding right now! You've got people running up the street! Hold on, I'll tell you what's going on.

The whole building just exploded some more, the whole top part! The building's not intact! People are running up the street! Am I still connected?

People are running out.

Joe? Joe! There's been another explosion now...

Oh my gosh!

...at the World Trade Center.

Oh! Oh my God!

This is on the right-hand side?

Yeah. Oh! Oh my gosh. The entire building... it looks like the side of the building has collapsed. Oh my gosh, this is horrific, absolutely horrific. How could that have happened? How could that have happened unless there was some sort of secondary explosion within those planes? Now this, uh, Ed, was the World Trade Center Two. Oh my gosh! This is…this is absolutely…

Uh, Joe, we can't…I can't tell from my perspective, eh…exactly what's…what's happened here…how much of the building is still standing.

But…but…but…but…Ed…but Ed…it looks like the side portion of that has totally fallen and there is just a huge cloud of dust that is encompassing several city blocks. Oh God…eh…eh…what… this…this…would…this would fall into the area of Lower Manhattan toward, uh, the eastern portion of the World Trade Center. It looks…now…uh…eh… is that? I'm trying to look… Can you see? Is that building still there?

I…I can't tell.

I don't see it!

I don't see the building because there's an awful lot of thick smoke.

Oh!

Ed, it doesn't look like the building is there!

I can't see because of the thick smoke so I don't know the answer to that, Joe, but it does not appear… and the only thing I can see is that police helicopter overhead… That smoke is so thick it has now drifted off to Lower Manhattan to the East River.

Oh! Ed?

We just received word that the south tower has collapsed!

OK.

Wow.

The. South. Tower. Has. Collapsed.

You'd almost think there was some type of

secondary explosion..

Ugh! Oh! I mean that's…that's…that's…

That would…that would…that would… And you have to wonder how that…

Let's just think about this logically.

There is no logic.

Oh my God!

…uh…uh…a hijacked air…air…airliner.

The scene, I mean, Ed, Ed…I mean, it's…it's horrific. Clouds and clouds of dust for blocks and blocks. Oh! I mean, people who were on the street near that building, um, are…are definitely in peril. It…it…it…you probably can't even breathe right now just given the amount of smoke. This…this building is collapsed!

This smoke, Joe, is now so thick. You're…you're correct. The building has collapsed! It's gone as much as eight to ten city blocks, so I can't see the top of any of the other buildings down there at all. That's how thick the smoke is.

Oh!

Oh my gosh! Oh my gosh! I… I… I… You're listening to special coverage of what is a catastrophic, um, day. This is beyond belief that the United States, uh, could be under attack. The Pentagon attack, now the south tower of the World Trade Center, um, has collapsed with, I'm sure, enormous, enormous loss of life.

There are two different types of smoke. First, that grayish-black smoke that was burning from the top of the Trade Center. Then, I would say below seventy stories, it's all white, which means there's been some type of collapse and debris.

Oh my gosh! This is terrible and, um, as we heard earlier… Alright, we're just getting something else here, Ed. Police are advising people who live in Lower Manhattan, such as Battery Park City, to try to evacuate as soon as possible although…

Try to evacuate.

Yes, I mean, this, um, I'm sure they fear other explosions but, um, this…this…this…debris and…and smoke… I'm not quite sure how far the debris has… has spread but, uh, the collapse has encompassed much of lower Manhattan. If…if you wanted to sort of put a landmark in…in your head…in your face…you're facing Lower Manhattan, you're facing two World Trade Center towers on the west side of Manhattan, World Trade Center One, the one with the tower, the one closest to the Hudson River is still standing, billowing from smoke. The second one has, uh, disappeared or, uh, the top portion has disappeared in this huge, huge cloud of, uh, smoke, white, black, yellow and it's…it's…it's…that sort of, uh… The collapse is spreading towards the eastern and southern portion of Manhattan and a huge cloud has just enveloped a lower part of the city and, uh, God help anybody who is in that area.

I don't know about you, Joe, but I got the shakes.

Uh, we…we should point out that the…we do have confirmation that the east building has collapsed. Is it building Two that has collapsed?

Yes, tower Two, the south tower has collapsed. The south tower has collapsed.

The amount of smoke, which has billowed, reaches as high, as does the still-burning tower One.

Well, oh boy, oh boy! This is, uh, this is, uh… it's not over yet and you know what? Un…un… unfortunately this is just going to get, um, worse and worse throughout the day as we get a closer look at the devastation that has been wrought on, uh, New York City and Washington and…and…and America in general as the smoke continues, uh, to billow out of the, uh, World Trade Center One, the one that is still standing. And the, uh, dust is still, um, rising into the air from the collapse of the south, uh, World Trade Center building. It's just a, uh, eh, it's…it's…it's…this is a day that will live in infamy.

Yeah, you're…you're…right. That's, um, not overstating it… The morning of this day…the 11th of September, 2001… will live in infamy. There's almost no textbook for any of us here on the radio to figure out just what to say. There are no words at all to express this.

III.

Everybody here is panicking. There's a huge crowd outside. There are hundreds of people on the streets that come from south to north. I mean literally thousands of people have been running from inside these building. It's a very heavily trafficked area in downtown. Many of them were inside the building when they felt the explosion. And they say there was just pandemonium—no warning, no alarms, no anything. Everyone just raced from their desks, ran downstairs and now there is a steady stream of folks running away from the building, fearing that there will be another collapse. And when they saw the second plane, they were convinced that this was dangerous. There is an actual flood of folks escaping downtown, midtown Manhattan right now. Right now, honestly, there are scores of people literally running behind me. There is debris on the base of the building that has continued to fall, as you know, as far as several blocks away from the building. And what's happened is everyone seems to have figured out that there's ongoing danger, and there's just a stream of folks running as quickly as they can uptown away from this.

IV.

What's that sound? There's another sound! Something is happening! There's a big sound! I don't know what this says...

It appears that...it appears, again there is a lot of smoke... It appears that the remainder of the World Trade Center tower has collapsed to the ground!

We're in the worst place we can be. We can't see a thing!

It's gone! Are you saying it's gone?

It's gone! It's gone! We can't see anything! All this smoke is moving and there's no towers standing there anymore.

We do have confirmation, that the, the north tower...has collapsed.

Oh, yes, it's not there!

It is not there.

It is not there.

People are running up Broadway again. Whatever was left has now...

We just heard another big explosion it sounded like a subway rumbling, but louder. And suddenly we looked up and it had come down! So then I got in my stomach, like, this knot, like, oh my God, oh my God, when? And where? Am I going to hear it? Or see? Or feel it?

Oh God!

Indeed, nothing remains. Virtually nothing remains of the two World Trade Center towers. There are no World Trade Center towers at this moment.

There's smoke coming up lower Broadway. You can't see the Brooklyn Bridge. We can't see anything but what we can tell you is that there are no towers standing. I would presume that this latest explosion that we heard and all the smoke was caused from the tower coming down. Did it sound like an explosion or perhaps the sound of collapsing building materials? Can you differentiate?

It did…it did…you know, you know, when they tear down a building, you know, a building that's been planned to come down…and you hear that explosion sound? It almost sounded like that or like the rumble of the subway.

There's somebody standing here with me right now. Come here. Tell us your name.

David Donovan.

I see you're covered with…

…smoke, dust, dirt, you name it. I was on the eighty-seventh floor and, uh, something hit. Uh, we didn't know exactly what it was when we were coming down. Somebody said it was a plane. Two planes at the building. We walked down eighty-seven floors. As we were coming out, uh, the first roof collapsed and I lost everybody. I don't know where anyone is. All I heard was the building shake and it filled up with smoke and fire. We didn't know what to do. We were going to stay there and then finally we got too much smoke and it took about fifteen minutes to start walking.

As you stand there right now…

…I'm shaking.

Can you believe it?

I…I can't. I just see dust. This is insane. I'm shaking. I'm covered in dust and stone. My clothes are all ripped.

The World Trade Center has been virtually eliminated to nothing by virtue of these terrorist attacks this morning. Two buildings are not in evidence as I sit and look at what is the outline of half a moon just over, uh, midtown Manhattan.

La…ladies and gentlemen, the World Trade Center buildings are gone. The World Trade Center buildings are gone. They are ashes. And, um, it's…it's…it is a situation beyond description.

V.

…and who were there because they were working when this attack occurred describe it as a "war zone." One fire marshal, a gentleman by the name of Mike Smith says everyone was screaming, crying, running, cops, people, firefighters, everyone. One businessman said, I just saw the building I work in come down. And that of course is the World Trade Center, which is…which has just collapsed in clubble…uh…in rubble behind him. Dust and dirt is everywhere and it still is everywhere covering, uh, nearly all of Lower Manhattan, ashes two to three inches deep in places, uh, people were wandering around, just dazed and terrified. It a horrifying, horrifying picture. Karen?

And President Bush has called it both a terrorist attack and a national tragedy. Attacks on American landmarks with American Airlines airplanes. We have the two Trade Towers coming down, we have a plane flying into the Pentagon, which has been evacuated and is still burning at this hour, and we also have a report of a plane down—a large plane—in Western Pennsylvania, a 767. The FAA is also still trying to locate several planes that are still missing and may be hijacked. Officials also say it is still too soon to speculate who may have been behind this. Palestinian leader Yasser Arafat has denied responsibility, condemned it and has called it unbelievable, unbelievable, unbelievable. Jim?

The, uh, the stories that, uh, people are now telling about, uh, what happened this morning are…are now coming and the eyewitnesses are telling, um, oh, these horrifying stories. People, before the two buildings collapsed, uh, jumping out of windows, uh, falling to their deaths, uh, trying to escape, the burning, uh, plane and the…and the smoke. One, uh, eyewitness, uh, a man by the name of Kenny Johanamen, uh, tells us what…what he saw when when he was, uh, in in the building… Uh, eh, do we have Kenny? Apparently we don't have Kenny Johanamen there. Kenny, eh, said that he was in the basement, ah, apparently of the World Trade Center, uh, when the building just came down and the elevator just blew up. There was lots… lots of smoke. He says, I dragged a guy out, his skin was hanging off. I dragged him out and I helped him to the ambulance. For many other people, unfortunately, there was to be no help because both buildings collapsed upon them.

And recapping what we've told you, we have America under attack, a terrorist attack is what President Bush is calling it. Both World Trade Center towers have collapsed. The scene in New York is one of disbelief. Smoke is now obscuring the entire skyline of Manhattan. All fel…federal buildings in New York and Washington D.C. are closed. There have been attacks in Washington as well. We have a report of the Pentagon being struck by a plane, the fire is still burning there. There was a report of a car bomb outside of the State Department. That has since been shot down. We also have a report—we had a report—that there was a bomb at the Capitol Building, but that has since been, uh, shot down as well. Most of the, uh, federal buildings in Washington have been evacuated—the Treasury Department, the Capitol, even the White House, where reporters were hurriedly herded out of the building where a plane was circling overhead—are empty.

It's unclear who was responsible for these attacks and…and…that, um, will become clear in the weeks and months ahead but, uh, clearly this was a coordinated attack. It happened in rapid fire fashion, uh, one plane and then another, uh, into the World Trade Center in New York and then a third plane into the Pentagon in Washington and a fourth plane crashing in Pennsylvania. We believe it may be connected, we don't verify that yet. This all happened very quickly and the reports came in just as quickly.

We are boarding Air Force One. They have bomb squads out here checking all of our gear.

Here on Capitol Hill. We've just been told that the Capitol is being evacuated and that all reporters follow the…

America Under Attack. War coverage continues from WABC radio news. This is WABC, New York City.

It just blew up. A big explosion… People started running, it was chaos everywhere.

An eyewitness describing the scene in what used

to be the World Trade Center towers in New York City in Lower Manhattan. Both towers hit by airplanes this morning. We were told an American Airlines jet crashed into one of the towers, then incredibly, both one-hundred-ten-story towers collapsed. They crumbled, bodies falling from the buildings. American Airlines now says it lost two planes, around one hundred sixty people on board both of those planes. They are gone. New York City is closed down. Then in Washington, another plane crashed into the Pentagon.

This is one of those things that you dream of in your worst nightmares. It appears that a large jet aircraft, perhaps the size of a large passenger plane came, uh, very low, clipping off light posts as it approached the Pentagon and it slammed into the side of the Pentagon and it drove itself from the outer ring all the way to the inner ring. The area of the building that it went into burst into flames. Um, there are many, many floors of destruction, deep into the heart of the Pentagon.

No casualty numbers yet but they're sure to be very high. Another large plane has crashed in southeastern Pennsylvania in Somerset County. Apparently that may be a United jet that was hijacked out of Chicago. The FBI is now trying to determine who is responsible for today's attacks. All planes are grounded around the country.

A gargantuan explosion! Oh my God! I don't believe it!

An eyewitness to an unbelievable disaster in the past hour. A plane apparently hit one of the towers of the World Trade Center in Lower Manhattan in New York.

America Under Attack. Our coverage continues. WABC News. This is WABC, New York City.

VI.

Airliners do not fly into the World Trade Center. I mean, it just doesn't happen unless they are directed that way by its pilot. Obviously this is not something that's accidental. I think it's interesting, too, that Manhattan island is completely locked down.

We're locked down. Those of us who are on Manhattan can't get off and those of us who are not on this island cannot get on. And for good reason: they've shut down virtually every major transit route onto or off of the island. And it almost reminds me of February of 1993, where there was the first act of terrorism directed at the World Trade Center, when the Ryder van that rolled into a parking lot there with fifteen hundred pounds of nitrate explosives, took out five floors, rocked the foundation, close to half a dozen deaths, thousands of injuries, but the building was able to withstand that blast and stay tall. In this particular case, John Gambling, both towers collapsed almost within a half an hour of each other.

I'm not, uh, a construction expert, but it just seems to me that that was awfully rapid for it to have been the result of just the airplane crashes and the fire. Although the fires were very intense, obviously, fueled by the jet fuel that was on board both of those aircraft.

I think the other thing that we have to understand here is that this is the first time in American history that our government has really gone into exile. I mean, our government at the moment, is in control and they're controlling things and they're…and they're… discussing, um, everything, but they are in exile.

Is it okay if a few of us start to assume that is a terrorist attack?

Well, you know, you can assume it. But I don't agree, based on what G.W. Bush is talking about.

He is the President of the United States, Ron.

I know that, but he's not often the most well informed guy around, Bill.

Well, but right now you would think he would be locked in to the information pipeline.

You would think.

And you would even hope. I'm just not assuming, Bob.

I think it's fair to say that people in the Middle East have declared America to be the big Satan and...

Wait! Not only have we called them terrorists, but now we're pointing fingers, okay?

Well, excuse me, Ron. Who had targeted the World Trade Center before?

I remember when the Murrah building went up and for a day and a half everybody was talking about, yes, the terrorist cells right there in Oklahoma, a hotbed of Middle Eastern Arabic activity. Nobody doubted these were Arab terrorists who blew up the Murrah Building. Well, it turned out to be blond-haired, blue-eyed, corn-fed country boys.

Ron, can we talk probabilities, though? Is it more likely this might have had something to do with the Middle East than it does with the Michigan Militia? Wouldn't it be more likely?

Well, that would've been the case in the Murrah Federal Building, too. It absolutely would have been more likely that terrorists blew up the Federal Building in Oklahoma when it was in fact a bunch of neo-Nazis.

Ron, as you know, in radical Muslim literature, they refer to New York City as sort of the Jewish capital of the world, even larger in scope than Tel Aviv.

Well, certainly the Twin Towers were specific targets of the original bombing and they specifically talked about the importance of hitting the Trade Center as a target of American wealth and power.

Lawrence Eagleburger, former Secretary of State, just said that this was a total intelligence breakdown and that with the magnitude of the attack he considers this a total act of war and that there hasn't been anything like this since Pearl Harbor. He equates this devastation to Pearl Harbor and said that basically only Osama bin Laden would have the capacity to coordinate this. He says an attack like this takes months or years to coordinate and that's why, he says, there was a total breakdown in our intelligence. He also pointed out the obvious, that we thought that we had licked hijacking in this country and apparently, at least, it appears on the surface that we have not licked hijacking. Whether they had weapons or if they just rushed the cockpit or whatever, if they did that it still remains a possibility here in the United States. So, Lawrence Eagleburger said that George Bush needs to respond quickly and go after terrorism wherever terrorism exists, indicating that even if we don't know for sure that they were the people directly responsible, we must go after those who support Osama bin Laden and who have done so in the past.

Well, so Lawrence Eagleburger advocated attacking who?

Well, he said our first target should be Osama bin Laden. He also talked about the Taliban and the government in Afghanistan. Uh, we have warned them, apparently according to him, through our State Department and through Washington that, should anything in the future occur against any American targets, they would be held responsible if bin Laden was implicated or found to be responsible.

We would have attacked Osama bin Laden already if we knew where he was.

Well, that's what I was just going to bring up. Several weeks ago, maybe several months ago—you know the way time flies—I remember saying on the air that Osama bin Laden was handing out promotional videotapes to the media. Osama bin Laden was interviewed by I don't know which network but that means they...

But you're saying we know where he is.

Well, they...we have to know where he is.

Well, I don't think he's having a news conference today.

No, not today.

Well, I don't know where he is. I don't know that he's responsible, with all due respect to former Secretary of State Eagleburger, if this was a matter of three people coordinating hijacking of three planes, you don't need a huge infrastructure and a lot of money. This was not a particularly hi-tech terrorist attack, although it was obviously a very well coordinated and very well planned one, but you don't need one hundred, two hundred people. You don't need...

But Ron, Afghanistan has consistently given sanctuary to Osama bin Laden and his minions. They have been warned about this, not just by the United States but internationally, and also by some of their fellow Muslim countries who also fear Osama bin Laden because of his radical fundamentalist ways. And if you're providing a base, a haven, a sanctuary for a terrorist who has targeted the United States and Israel, well then, you're just as culpable because you do nothing to sort of relieve yourself of that.

Again. We've made a leap here that I don't think is justified in making yet, which is we've assigned blame to Osama bin Laden.

Well, I can bet you he's got a big smile on his face right now.

Yeah. Either way, he's probably happy, but you can't kill a guy for being happy.

Oh, actually given the way I feel right now you probably could.

Well, maybe you should just take the day off.

I'm not a huge fan of U.S. military power, but it would be nice to see aircraft or a military jet sort of flying around the perimeter of Manhattan.

Absolutely. You'd expect to see that at any moment. You'd expect to see U.S. military flying around the World Trade Center and also perhaps the Empire State Building or any other monument that we have.

Well, in fact, the only times we've ever had airline crashes or planes crashing into buildings here in New York—obviously there are very high buildings and planes are constantly flying overhead—is in times of fog. But today is…

…a clear day. Blue sky. That's not what this is.

Couldn't be, even if navigation systems failed.

I'm appalled at, uh, what we're gonna find out as the day goes on in terms of the loss of life. It is going to be dramatic and, um, you know what? With all due respect to the president, it's not good enough to say, at this point, we're gonna hunt them down and find those responsible. I mean we got to get them and get them fast.

I've just been trying to think back. After Pearl Harbor there were about two thousand, twenty-five hundred American casualties on American soil. Uh, there were a couple of instances, I believe, in California during World War II—more accidental than anything else—where there were some people who were killed, but that's it. This country has remained impervious to this sort of attack ever since that time.

All of that has ended today.

I said earlier that this is a day that will live in infamy. This is...this is one horrific day. And given the enormity of the situation, the organization of these attacks, Ed, this is not one lunatic. Right away we're gonna think Osama bin Laden, maybe Osama bin Laden is behind this, and if he is, then, he's gonna get it. But you know what? It isn't one man. It isn't Osama bin Laden and a couple of cronies in some tent somewhere in Northern Africa or wherever. This is an organized attack against the United States which can only be state-sponsored terrorism. This isn't one lunatic with a lot of money doing anything on the scale that we are seeing unfold before our eyes here today in New York and around the nation.

You're right, Joe. The instinct for bloodlust, for retribution is extraordinarily strong. They may not be done.

VII.

George Weber is near the scene of the World Trade Center now. George? Tell us what you know at the moment.

Bruce I've now moved a good way east, I guess,

out of sheer curiosity. A giant plume of black and white smoke is blowing across downtown. This afternoon, they're not letting reporters anywhere close to the area where the two World Trade towers collapsed earlier today. I'm standing right next to the Manhattan Bridge, which is one of the entry points where they're bringing in ambulances and emergency personnel. We still periodically see some U.S. military aircraft doing flybys. This is the sound that you hear…hour after hour down here.

And just below me is a park right near the edge of Chinatown. And while there's some curiosity among these people, they continue to play their card games. They continue to chat as if nothing is going on. Their markets are open. They're shopping, they're…they're… they're buying their fish. Uh, it's…it's as if this little corner of New York City was totally unaffected, but you know it's at the top of their minds. They're talking about it. They're pointing up in the air periodically and they're continuing with their card games. So it's, uh, just a little snapshot of, uh, a piece of New York as they deal with this immense tragedy.

Michael Jackson

I.

Wow, it's weird cause, uh, I'm hearing this music and I'm seeing online this video of the three Charlie's Angels running out of a door, you know. Uh oh. Jeff McKinney's running into the room.

Well, much talk today about Farrah Fawcett certainly, but now there is news that Michael Jackson has been rushed to a hospital, um, I think it's in Los Angeles, I'm not sure. The CBS newsroom just came on saying that there is a special report coming up for Michael Jackson's physical condition, which apparently is, uh, dire at this moment.

It's so interesting. Before we came on the air today—I hope this is not the case—but Jimmy and I were talking about how things happen in threes. We just lost Ed McMahon, today we lose Farrah Fawcett, now we're hearing Jeff McKinney walking in telling us...

I'm saying he's ill. I'm saying he's ill. I don't know how dire he is but the indication is that he is quite ill. They're gonna run a special report. They don't do that lightly, the folks back in New York. So we're gonna do this in about ten seconds here. We're gonna get the latest on Michael Jackson.

Boy, there's a lot, a lot of curiosity here.

Alright so let's take it away. It's four fifteen.

This is a CBS News special report. I'm Dan Raviv. We are receiving word from Los Angeles that the pop superstar Michael Jackson has been rushed to a hospital. The Los Angeles Times website says it got some confirmation from the L.A. Fire Department that Michael Jackson was not breathing when paramedics arrived and took him to the hospital. Let's go to the CBS newsroom in Los Angeles. Correspondent Steve Futterman, what are you learning?

Dan, we're just hearing these reports, still nothing confirmed. Reportedly Michael Jackson has been taken to the UCLA Medical Center, which is not far from his home, but nothing official yet from the UCLA Medical Center. According to the L.A. Times, Captain Steve Ruda, who's with the L.A. Fire Department says that paramedics responded to a call at Jackson's home around twelve twenty-six local time—that's just under two hours ago. According to the Times, he was not breathing when they arrived. The paramedics, according to the newspaper, performed CPR and took him to the UCLA Medical Center. The website TMZ says that Jackson was in cardiac arrest and that paramedics administered CPR in the ambulance. According to TMZ, Michael Jackson's mother is on the way or may be there already at the UCLA hospital to visit him. But again, we want to emphasize that there has been no official confirmation. Two reports, one from the L.A. Times, one from the website TMZ, both of them saying that Michael Jackson has been taken to a hospital.

Jackson, by the way, is age fifty. This comes on the same day that the actress and star Farrah Fawcett died of cancer in Los Angeles at age sixty-two. CBS News special report. I'm Dan Raviv.

Okay. So as far as we know, Michael Jackson is still alive but there are two reports saying that he was in cardiac arrest when, uh, EMTs got to him and they were administering CPR as they rushed Michael Jackson to the hospital. Shocking to hear that Michael Jackson is fifty years old.

I was just thinking of that. We were talking earlier about how, you know, it seems like yesterday we were watching Farrah Fawcett in her youth and beauty—and sixty-two years old to me is still young—you don't think of Farrah Fawcett being sixty-two years old. You don't think of Michael Jackson as being fifty. It's... it's just strange.

There's some real parallels between these two people— Farrah Fawcett and Michael Jackson—in that they both had overwhelming, huge effects of popularly in their heyday.

Um hum. Um hum.

I mean, Michael Jackson did have the same sort of...different effect, but he had the same sort of all-encompassing effect on...on the world as Farrah Fawcett did, you know?

When he...when he was at his height...

...1983, 1984...

...his peak, it was like nothing you'd ever seen. I mean, it was...

But you could say the same for Farrah Fawcett, though.

Yeah, you could. I...I think it's...yeah, you're right. You could. You absolutely could say the same thing for her. And then she went and married, uh, Steve Majors? Steve Majors? Remember she became Farrah Fawcett.

Six Million Dollar...Lee Majors.

Yeah. Lee Majors. Why did I think it was Steve Majors? Next thing you know I'll say Paul Majors, but no it was Lee Majors.

Farrah Fawcett herself as well, I mean, there is, you know, in... in her heyday...

For a brief period of time...

Excuse me?

For a brief period of time she had at least, domestically...she was about as famous as you can get within the confines of the United States of America.

Absolutely. Charlie's Angels was the biggest hit on television. That poster, the famous poster of her...

The poster, yeah.

...was the biggest seller. I mean, she did...she did a spread for Playboy in the 90s and that was the biggest selling issue of the decade. I mean, she was a big star as well.

Do you know what kinds of health problems Michael Jackson had?

I didn't know he had any.

He has had occasional fainting attacks and things like that. We've always heard that. I mean, he's certainly never looked robust, Michael Jackson, to say the least.

No.

But I think this is the first indication we...we've ever had that Michael Jackson has any sort of serious health issues and this appears to be a very serious health issue.

Two updates that have come to TMZ here in the last few minutes. A Jackson family member tells TMZ that Michael is in, quote, really bad shape and that the brothers are now headed to UCLA.

Well, that sounds very unofficial, of course.

Yes. And then there's another update from TMZ saying that they've just got off the phone with Joe Jackson—that's the father, Michael's dad—who says he is, quote, not doing well.

OK.

So?

So, Farrah Fawcett has died, the great superstar of the seventies. And now, the great superstar of the eighties—equaling her superstardom—there are reports, that he has been in cardiac arrest this afternoon and has been rushed to the hospital in Los Angeles. So, stay tuned, I guess. We'll continue to get news throughout the day on that.

There are probably at least a thousand people outside the hospital right now where he is in Los Angeles. Evidently, they're gathering and they're in a perfect rectangle, I guess holding a... some sort of séance?

Not a séance. A, uh, vigil.

Well, a séance would make more sense for him. He's got plenty of eccentricities, but the music…

Well, he doesn't have anywhere close to the talent Elvis had.

We're not talking about talent. We're talking about influence.

I'm just saying that Elvis's influence overshadows his by 100 times.

I…I don't know about that.

I do.

Well, OK, I'm saying between 1980 and 1990, I mean, doesn't he have like five of the all time top ten records sold?

Jeff. Jeff. There are still people who want to sound like Elvis! There's nobody who wants to sound like Michael Jackson. Not the impersonators. I'm talking about real bands, I mean, you know, not Elvis impersonators.

Elvis will be impersonated for another hundred years.

It's got nothing to do with impersonation. You've got real rock bands out there who still love Elvis and are trying to do music like Elvis. Without Elvis, is there rock 'n' roll? You know? What is Michael Jackson responsible for? What did he come up with that's so special?

He created a video channel, essentially. If not for Michael Jackson videos, MTV wouldn't be on and what it is today.

So we can blame him for that.

On the other hand, the Jackson Five…

Ladies and gentlemen, please welcome up on stage, the Jackson Four!

It doesn't have the same ring.

No, it doesn't.

Well, this is gonna be a bizarre day if this story continues to develop. I mean, if he stabilizes, we can all sort of breathe a sigh of relief and say…

…speaking of which, did you hear that the World Climatological Society has issued a, uh, wind alert this afternoon?

No.

Yeah, all of the children across the world let out a collective sigh of relief.

I've got more! I've got more!

That's enough.

What a week! Ed McMahon, Farrah Fawcett...

...and Michael Jackson.

Uh, guys. He's still with us. He's, uh...

...as far as we know.

II.

This is a CBS news special report. I'm Dan Raviv. About an hour after first word that pop music star Michael Jackson suffered a heart attack in Los Angeles, it's now reported and, reliably reported, that he has died. The Los Angeles Times website says Michael Jackson, age fifty, has died. He was in a coma when taken from an expensive rental home in Los Angeles. The website TMZ.com has also been reporting that Jackson died. We go live to Los Angeles. CBS news correspondent Steve Futterman.

Well, Dan, if all this is correct, it's just a shock here in Southern California and around the world. The L.A. Times, as you said, saying that, uh, Michael Jackson was pronounced dead—this is according to the L.A. Times—by doctors this afternoon after arriving at the hospital in a deep coma. The L.A. Times is quoting city and law enforcement sources. The L.A. Times, uh, a very reliable newspaper. Obviously the website TMZ, which also has been very reliable in the past, had earlier reported that Jackson had died. Now we had reports confirmed by Los Angeles Fire Department Captain Steve Ruda that Jackson was not breathing when paramedics arrived at his home. All this began around three hours ago, that's when the 911 call was made, exactly three hours ago. Paramedics came to the home—that's when Jackson reportedly was not breathing—and was taken to the UCLA Medical

Center. Now, as we've heard, both the Los Angeles Times and TMZ are reporting that Michael Jackson, the pop star, the legendary pop star, known by millions of fans around the world, has died.

Steve Futterman reporting live from CBS News in Los Angeles. Michael Jackson was fifty years old. Here's a look back at his career from CBS's Dave Browde.

They called him the King of Pop. At least his fans did. But that nickname was his publicist's invention, a kind of tabloid label for the prodigiously talented but, bizarrely behaving, superstar. They called him Wacko Jacko. Michael Jackson, the son of an Indiana steelworker who'd started an astonishing show business career at the age of five as the lead singer of the Jackson Five, the group featuring Michael and four of his brothers. The Jackson Five turned out fourteen albums of hits. Michael broke out with four solo discs. But he truly became a superstar and thrilled the world in 1982. Michael Jackson's Thriller broke all records, selling some fifty million copies worldwide. Jackson broke more new ground in the then-fledgling music video field with his fourteen-minute Thriller video, in which Jackson began displaying the remarkable dance skills that would again launch his career over the moon. But Jackson's increasingly reclusive and bizarre behavior—along with his reported multiple plastic surgeries—made tabloid headlines surpassing his sales, as did an incident in which his hair caught fire during the 1984 filming of a soda commercial. Then there was Jackson's purchase of the ranch he called Neverland, which he stocked with animals, amusement park rides, and a constant flow of children. Suddenly, swirling accusations exploded. In 1993, Jackson released a video denial that he'd molested a thirteen-year-old boy who visited Neverland.

These statements about me are totally false.

Jackson reportedly settled by paying the boy's family millions.

Please welcome Mr. and Mrs. Michael Jackson.

Jackson's marriage to Lisa Marie Presley almost immediately thereafter, was seen by many as a desperate ploy to rehabilitate his image—it broke up after only nineteen months. Jackson's next album was a disappointment, despite a duet with superstar sister Janet. After another album—his first complete flop—Jackson married again to a nurse, Debbie Rowe. The couple had two children in as many years, followed quickly by divorce, fights with his record company, litigation over allegedly canceled appearances, and apparently, even more plastic surgery. Jackson explained his changing skin color as the result of a disease of vitiligo. Then, Jackson's most incredible public incident: dangling his eleven-month-old son, Prince, over a balcony, followed quickly by Jackson's arrest on charges of molesting a twelve-year-old cancer patient. Jackson's denial this time on 60 Minutes.

Totally false. If I would hurt a child, I would slit my wrists. I would never hurt a child.

Jackson's behavior while facing the criminal charges, redefined eccentricity. Jumping on his limo to delighted fans one day, showing up late in pajamas another. Ultimately, he was acquitted, but despite many loyal fans, his image was in tatters.

That's CBS's Dave Browde. If you've just tuned in, Michael Jackson, at age fifty, has died. He suffered a heart attack—an apparent heart attack—in Los Angeles. Michael Jackson died, yes, on the same day that Farrah Fawcett died of cancer in Los Angeles at age sixty-two. We turn to Anthony DeCurtis who has written about music for so many years for Rolling Stone magazine. Uh, Anthony, uh, indeed it's the music we should focus on because that...that's what will last.

Well, absolutely. I mean it's, you know, with all the scandals and all the problems and all the weirdness that Michael represented, you know, it's easy to lose sight of the music and the music is extraordinary. I mean, this is somebody who is as important a figure as popular music has produced.

And, just the way he went at age...at age fifty, I guess we realize there was something wrong with his health, with his behavior, or with the advice he got from others.